Landscapes of
WESTERN
CRETE

a countryside guide
Second edition

Jonnie Godfrey
and
Elizabeth Karslake

SUNFLOWER
BOOKS

Revised printing 1994
Second edition 1991
Sunflower Books
12 Kendrick Mews
London SW7 3HG

ISBN 0-948513-98-5

Century plant
or American
aloe (Agave
americana)

Important note to the reader ⸺

We have tried to ensure that the descriptions in this book are error-free at press date. The book will be up-dated, where necessary, whenever future printings permit. We would be grateful to receive any comments — sent in care of the publishers, please.

We rely on walkers to take along a good supply of common sense — as well as this book — on their rambles. Conditions change fairly quickly on Crete, and **storm damage or roadworks could make a walk unsafe at any time.** If a route is not as we outline it, and your way ahead is not secure, return to the point of departure. **Do not attempt to complete a walk under hazardous conditions.** Please read carefully the notes on pages 38 to 45. Walk *safely*, while at the same time respecting the countryside. Always check for any STOP PRESS comments at the back of the book!

Photographs by Elizabeth Karslake
Maps by Pat Underwood
Drawings by Sharon Rochford
Printed and bound in the UK by The KPC Group, Ashford, Kent

6 5 4 3 2 1

🌻 Contents

Preface   5
Acknowledgements; Background reading   6

Getting about   7
Plans of Hania and Rethimnon   8-9
    city exits • bus departure points

Picnicking   10
Picnic suggestions   11

Touring   13
Some points worth noting   14

    THE CAR TOURS

    THE FAR WEST (TOUR 1)   15
      Hania • (Kasteli) • (Polirinia) • Sfinari • Vathi • Moni
      Chrisoskalitisas • (Elafonisi) • Elos • Topolia •
      Kaloudiana • Hania

    PALEOHORA AND SOUTH COAST BEACHES (TOUR 2)   19
      Hania • Tavronitis • Voukolies • Kandanos •
      Paleohora • Kandanos • (Sougia) • Hania

    **COUNTRYSIDE, COASTAL BACKWATER AND
    HIGH CRETAN PASTURELAND (TOUR 3)**   22
      Hania • Nea Roumata • Agia Irini • Epanohori •
      Sougia • Omalos • Laki • Fournes • Hania

    THE AKROTIRI PENINSULA (TOUR 4)   25
      Hania • Kounoupidiana • Kalathas • Stavros •
      Agia Triada • Moni Gouverneto • (Souda Bay
      Cemetery) • Hania

    **THE FOOTHILLS OF THE LEVKA ORI (THE WHITE
    MOUNTAINS) (TOUR 5)**   27
      Hania • Aptera • Katohori • Kambi • Mournies • Hania

    A SLICE OF CRETE (TOUR 6)   29
      Hania • Vrises • Askyfou • Hora Sfakion •
      Frangokastello • Selia • Moni Preveli • Rethimnon •
      Episkopi • Georgioupoli • Hania

    CRETAN TREASURES (TOUR 7)   34
      Hania • (Rethimnon) • Armeni • Spili • Agia Galini •
      Festos • Agia Triada • Hania

    THE AMARI VALLEY (TOUR 8)   35
      Hania • Rethimnon • Apostoli • Thronos • Fourfouras
      • Agios Ioannis • Gerakari • Rethimnon • Hania

3

alking 38
Guides, waymarking, maps 39
Things that bite or sting 40
What to take 40
Where to stay 41
Weather 41
Walkers' checklist 42
Greek for walkers 42
Organisation of the walks 44
A country code for walkers and motorists 45

THE WALKS

1 Kato Stalos • Agia Marina • Platanias 46
2 From coast to lake: Stalos to Agia 48
3 Theriso • Zourva • Meskla 50
4 Drakonas to Theriso 52
5 Katohori to Stilos or Nio Horio 54
6 Kambi • Volika refuge • Kambi 57
7 Georgioupoli circuit 62
8 Alikampos • Kournas lake • Georgioupoli 67
9 The Prassanos Gorge 69
10 Rethimnon • Agia Irini • Kapadiana • Chromonastiri • Myli • (Rethimnon) 74
11 Vrissinas, Minoan peak sanctuary 77
12 Gouverneto and Katholikou 78
13 The Rodopou Peninsula: Rodopos • Agios Ioannis Gionis • Rodopos 79
14 The Rodopou Peninsula: Rodopos • Moni Gonia • Kolimbari 84
15 Sirikari to Polirinia 87
16 Katsamatados • Mouri • Voulgaro 90
17 Sasalos • Katsamatados • Topolia 93
18 Sougia • Lisos • Paleohora 95
19 Xiloskala • Linoseli Col • Gingilos • Xiloskala 100
20 Xiloskala • Kallergi • Xiloskala 103
21 Kallergi • Mavri • Melindaou • Kallergi 106
22 The Samaria Gorge 109
23 Agia Roumeli to Loutro 112
24 Loutro to Hora Sfakion 115
25 The Imbros Gorge • Komitades • Hora Sfakion 118
26 Askyfou • Asfendos • Agios Nektarios 120
27 Plakias • Selia • The Kotsifas Gorge • Mirthios • Plakias 125
28 Fourfouras to Korakia (Ida range) and return 127

Bus timetables 131

Index (of geographical names) 133

Fold-out island map between pages 14 and 15

Drawings of island flora 1, 2, 45, 74-75, 128-129

STOP PRESS 135

❀ Preface

Mountains rearing straight up from the sea, deep wooded gorges, ravines and valleys — and yet more glorious mountains, standing proud and acting as a magnet to the eye and the imagination — that's western Crete, or real Crete, as some would say. Its strong, dramatic scenery and colours create sweeping landscapes of harsh but beautiful countryside — countryside that has been the backdrop for heroic deeds, ancient civilisations and constant intrigue for thousands of years, and the home of obdurate, tough people — made so by their labours on the land and their experiences.

Getting to know western Crete takes time, and there are still relatively few people who explore beyond the obvious. But we hope that by putting this book together we will lead you straight to the heart of the matter, whether you are someone who doesn't need convincing but simply wants a reliable and thorough guide, or if you are a first- or second-time visitor who wants to get to grips with the island but are unsure how to go about it. We hope we will not only introduce you to the region but encourage you to explore to the full. We won't need to inspire you; one look at western Crete will do that.

Landscapes of Western Crete, in the same tried and tested format as the other titles in the series, takes you well off the beaten track, while at the same time describing in full the most popular touring routes and excursions. This Second edition, as well as being a thorough update with new maps, includes five new walks, three of them based on Rethimnon.

Everyone has heard of the Samaria Gorge, and rightly so. But frankly, anyone who contemplates walking the gorge — a long and by no means unchallenging expedition — could accomplish a number of other walks in this book and gain a great amount of pleasure in alternative landscapes. What's more, walking just about anywhere else in western Crete will give the added bonus of solitude and perhaps an even greater feeling for the island and its people, who vary both in style and character from region to region.

Acknowledging the fact that western Crete attracts a number of visitors who choose to have more than one

5

base, or who don't feel obliged to return to their villa, hotel or apartment every night, we have described walks that can be linked and which cover a large expanse of the western end of the island. Western Crete lends itself to this arrangement very well. These walks start above the Samaria Gorge, in the awe-inspiring White Mountains — Levka Ori (even when they're not snow-capped, their peaks are a striking white, hence their name).

We have been asked often if and how western and eastern Crete differ from one another. In fact we naturally made the comparison ourselves in the course of compiling this second guide, having previously written *Landscapes of Eastern Crete*. The west is even more mountainous and less developed than the east, so there's less asphalt to contend with. The geography is such that walks tend to be longer and the terrain, on the whole, rougher in the west. And the people of western Crete are somewhat more reserved than their counterparts in the east. The attraction is none the less for these differences, and western Crete has its own captivating and entrancing character. You simply need to immerse yourself in the countryside to find out.

— JONNIE GODFREY

Acknowledgements

We would like to express our gratitude to the following people:

Antonis Pavlakis, whose generosity and willingness made all things possible and whose apartments on the beach at Stalos were a perfect base;

Gordon Beveridge, Cindy Selby, John Channon, Nigel Moor, Bernard Redshaw and Dimitris Bountrogiannis — for checking the walks;

Likourgos Dimotakis, Maria Kalorizikakis and Pandelis Efthinakis of Aptera Travel, Yiannis Yiakoumakis, Josef Schwemberger, Maria and Manolis Tsotsolakis, Ingemaj and Makis Tsontos, and the Angelaki family — for Cretan hospitality, which includes support, encouragement, sustenance, fetching, carrying and firm friendship;

Simply Crete, Meon Villas and CV Travel for valuable assistance with travel arrangements.

Background reading

Adam Hopkins: *Crete: Past, Present & Peoples*
John Bowman: *The Travellers' Guide: Crete*
Pat Cameron: *The Blue Guide: Crete*
Nikos Kazantzakis: *Zorba the Greek*
W Stanley Moss: *Illmet by Moonlight*
David MacNeil Doren: *The Winds of Crete*
Oleg Polunin: *The Concise Flowers of Europe*
John Fisher: *The Rough Guide to Crete*

✹ Getting about

Hiring a car is certainly the best way to get to know Crete. There's no denying that it's quite costly, but we hope that by giving you some good itineraries, you will be able to make the most of the island — and your car. Many of the tours we suggest will take you past the starting- and/or end-points of several walks. In fact, seeing the countryside from a car will encourage you, we hope, to go off the beaten track and into the hills with us, on foot.

Taxis are an alternative way to tour and, if shared, can be a reasonably-priced way to travel. Do agree a fare before you set out, if it's going to be an unmetered journey. Your holiday company's agent or representative will help you to find a driver who speaks English and who will be happy and proud to show off his island.

Organised excursions are good value; coaches eat up the kilometres while you sit back and watch it all go by.

One of the best ways of getting about is by **local bus.** Once you've done it for the first time, you'll realise it's economical, reliable and entertaining. You'll whizz along the highways and bumble through villages with a bus-eye view over the countryside. Use the local bus network to explore western Crete economically. The plans on the following pages show you where the bus stations are in Hania and Rethimnon. Timetables for buses covering the western half of the island are on pages 131-132. Note: **Please be sure to pick up a current bus timetable** at the station before you plan any excursions: the frequency of services changes with the seasons. For complete assurance, verify the times in advance by asking. If you are lucky, the officials at Hania bus station (where, incidentally, there is a left luggage facility) will tell you the number of the bus you want, but they won't know it themselves much in advance of departure. Arrive in good time, as buses leave promptly and sometimes even *earlier* than scheduled, particularly those that depart at the crack of dawn. Most tickets are bought at the depot before boarding, including those to Samaria (the 'Omalos' bus). If you *do* buy tickets on the bus, don't be confused if you get three per person for just one trip — they add up to the total. You can flag down buses en route, but they don't always stop. *Always* put your hand out, even at a bus stop.

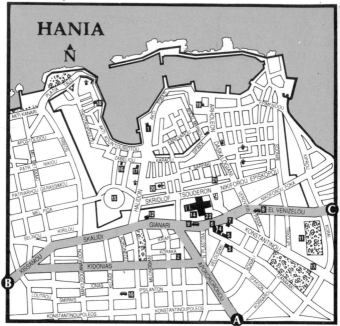

HANIA — KEY

1 Tourist information bureau
2 Tourist police
3 Olympic Airways terminal and Greek Alpine Club (EOS)
4 Post office
5 Telephone and telegraph (OTE)
6 National Bank of Greece
7 Bank of Greece
8 🚌 for Akrotiri
9 🚌 for Akrotiri, Iraklion, Souda, Mournies and town routes
10 🚌 for Alikianos, Aptera (beach), Hora Sfakion, Kalamaki,
   Kandanos, Kasteli, Laki, Meskla, Omalos (Samaria), Paleohora,
   Platanias (beach), Platanos, Rethimnon, Sougia, Xiloskala
   (Samaria)
11 Stadium
12 Ionian and Popular Bank
13 Public gardens and zoo
14 Market
15 Shivao bastion
16 Venetian loggia
17 Archaeological museum
18 Maritime museum (Firka tower)
19 Customs
20 Cathedral
21 Minaret
22 Hospital

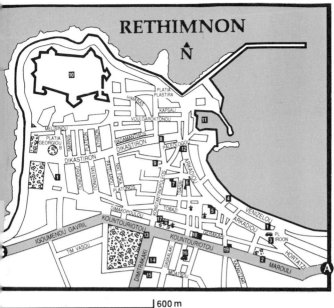

RETHIMNON — KEY

1 Tourist information bureau (two locations)
2 Post office
3 🚌 for Anogia, Amari
4 Public beach
5 Youth hostel
6 Greek Commercial Bank
7 National Bank of Greece
8 Arimondi fountain
9 Nerantzes fountain
10 Venetian fortress
11 Venetian harbour
12 Museum (Venetian loggia)
13 Public gardens
14 Fun fair
15 Bank of Greece
16 🚌 for Agia Galini, Fourfouras, Hania, Iraklion, Lefkogia, Plakias, Spili
17 🚖 taxi rank
18 Telephone and telegraph (OTE)
19 Town hall

✳ Picnicking

Picnicking on Crete is *not* an organised affair. There aren't any specially-provided sites; it's very much a case of pick your own olive tree and toss for the best view. So we can't tell you where there are tables and benches for picnickers; there aren't any. But following is a selection of some good places to throw down a towel or a rug (it's unlikely to be wet, but it might well be prickly) and revel in the countryside. Don't forget the corkscrew ... .

There are fourteen picnic suggestions. All have been chosen for ease of access and none involves too much climbing or lugging of provisions. All the information you need to get to these picnic places is given on the following pages, where *picnic numbers correspond to walk numbers.* (The three picnic suggestions on page 12, prefixed 'CT', are specifically linked to the corresponding *car tours.*) You can quickly find the general location on the island by looking at the pull-out touring map, where the area of each walk is outlined in white.

We include transport details (🚐 = how to get there by bus; 🚗 = where to leave your private transport), how long a walk you'll have, and setting or views. Beside the picnic title you'll find a map reference: the exact location of the picnic spot is shown on this *walking* map by the symbol *P*, and 🚐 and 🚗 symbols indicate the nearest bus and car access.

Finally, to help you choose a place that appeals to you, picture references are given for each picnic spot, where possible. Note that these aren't always photographs of the *exact* picnic place, but have been selected to illustrate the general scenery in the area.

If you're travelling to your picnic by bus, be sure to arm yourself with an up-to-date bus timetable. There are bus timetables on pages 131-132, but *do* remember that no book can ever be as up-to-date as the timetables you can obtain at bus stations.

If you are travelling to your picnic by car, be extra vigilant off the main roads; children and animals are often in the village streets. Without damaging plants, do park *well off* the road; *never* block a road or track.

All picnickers should read the country code on page 45 and go quietly in the countryside.

3 VIEWS FROM THERISO (map pages 52-53)

🚗 by car: about 10 minutes on foot. Use the touring map to drive to Theriso, south of Hania, in the foothills of the White Mountains (you are also near Theriso if you follow Car tour 3). Once at Theriso, use the notes on page 50 to drive along the track that Walk 3 follows — as far as the bridge (the 10min-point in the walk). Park here, well off the track, and then follow the path referred to in the walking notes for some 5-15 minutes.
🚌 by bus: about 20 minutes on foot. Use notes for Walk 3, page 50, climbing the path above the watercourse as far as you like.
While there is no photograph of this particular setting, the general landscape in the area is illustrated on page 50.

5a VIEWS FROM KATOHORI (map pages 58-59)

🚗 by car: under five minutes on foot. Follow Car tour 5. Coming down-hill into Katohori, on a big U-bend to the right (where there is a miniature concrete church), take the concrete track to the left. Continue, and park in the small square *(before* the bridge). Follow Walk 5, page 54.
🚌 by bus: some 15 minutes on foot. Use the notes for Walk 5, page 54.
Both setting and views are illustrated on page 56.

5b PICNIC IN A GORGE NEAR KATOHORI (map page 58-59)

🚗 by car: some 15 minutes on foot. Park as for Picnic 5a above, then follow the notes for Walk 5, to picnic in the waymarked gorge.
🚌 by bus: some 30 minutes on foot. Follow Walk 5, page 54.
This setting is illustrated on page 55.

6 KAMBI (map pages 58-59)

🚗 by car: about 10 minutes on foot. Follow Car tour 5, and park in Kambi. Then use the notes on page 57 (Walk 6) for 10-15 minutes.
🚌 by bus: about 10 minutes on foot. See page 57 (Walk 6).
The photograph on page 60 shows a similar setting and outlook.

8 KOURNAS LAKE (map pages 64-65)

🚗 by car: up to ten minutes on foot. Follow Car tour 6, page 33. Having passed the lake at Kournas, park near the bridge and walk to the lake.
🚌 by bus: some 45 minutes on foot. Take a bus to Georgioupoli (Timetables 1, 2); then follow Walk 8 in reverse.

10a VIEWS OVER RETHIMNON (map pages 70-71)

🚗 by car: no walking. Car tours 6, 7, and 8 take you to Rethimnon. From Rethimnon drive to the chapel of Profitis Ilias above the town. To get there, head south uphill on Theotokopoulou Street (at the eastern side of the town; this is the road to Roussospiti). Turn right into the track to the church and park. After enjoying the views, you may wish to walk on to the picnic setting described under 10b below.
🚌 by bus: about 20-25 minutes on foot. Follow the notes for Walk 10, page 74.

10b PICNIC IN THE PINES (map pages 70-71)

🚗 by car: up to 25 minutes on foot. Park as for Picnic 10a above. Then use the notes on page 74 to walk from Profitis Ilias to the pine woods not far above the chapel (25 minutes from Rethimnon; 5 minutes from the chapel).
🚌 by bus: 25 minutes on foot. Use the notes for Walk 10 (page 74) to go to Profitis Ilias and then on to the pine woods.

15 POLIRINIA (map pages 88-89)

🚗 by car: some 20-25 minutes on foot. Follow Car tour 1 and take the detour to Polirinia (page 16, paragraph 3). Park near the taverna at the end of the road and follow notes for Walk 15, but in reverse.

🚌 by bus: some 20-25 minutes on foot. Ask in Kasteli about buses to Polirinia; current (inconvenient) times are 07.30,14.00 *weekdays*. Then follow the notes for Walk 15 (page 87), but in reverse.
This picnic setting is shown on page 86.

16 KATSAMATADOS (map page 89)

🚗 by car: under 10 minutes on foot. Follow Car tour 1 to Katsamatados, 3km south of Topolia. Then use notes on page 90 (Walk 16) to picnic near the start of the walk.

🚌 by bus: under 10 minutes on foot. Follow Walk 16, page 90.
There is no close-up photograph of this setting, but the photograph on page 91 looks down on the picnic place from a ridge above it.

18 SOUGIA (map pages 96-97)

🚗 by car: some 10-15 minutes on foot. Follow Car tour 3 and park in Sougia, then use the notes for Walk 18 on page 95.

🚌 by bus: some 10-15 minutes on foot. See page 95 (Walk 18).
This picnic setting is illustrated on page 99.

25 IMBROS GORGE (map page 121)

🚗 by car: about 20 minutes on foot. Follow Car tour 6 to Imbros and park in the village. Then use notes on page 118 (Walk 25).

🚌 by bus: some 20 minutes on foot. Use notes page 118 (Walk 25).
This picnic setting is shown on page 118.

CT4 MONI GOUVERNETO (touring map, or map page 82)

🚗 by car: about 5-10 minutes on foot. Follow Car tour 4 to the Gouverneto Monastery and park. There are good picnic places on the hillside below the monastery, overlooking the sea, but little shade.
This picnic setting is illustrated on page 24.

CT6 KOURTALIOTIS GORGE (touring map)

🚗 by car: 5 minutes down on foot; 10 minutes back up. Follow Car tour 6 and, beyond Asomatos, turn right. You'll soon be heading up the Kourtaliotis Gorge. Look for railings and small signs on the right. You can park just in front of them. Walk down to the church and the waterfall.
Note: If you're staying at Plakias, this picnic is also accessible by bus; ask for the Kourtaliotis Gorge and waterfall.

CT8 AMARI VALLEY (touring map)

🚗 by car: under five minutes on foot. Follow Car tour 8, to cross the River Platys (125.5km). Park well off the road; picnic by the bridge.
This picturesque bridge by the Platys is shown on page 72.

One of the many hundreds of churches and chapels you might see in western Crete: this one is at Astratigos on the Rodopou Peninsula.

❀ Touring

Crete is a very large island, and most visitors hire a car for some part of their stay to get to grips with it. It pays to hire for a minimum of three days and, although you may find cheaper rates with small companies, do think what you're paying for with the better-known firms. The larger companies offer the advantage of representation all over the island. Since it's likely that you'll want to cover a lot of ground, you'll be in a better position hiring from a well-known company, should anything go wrong en route.

Remember that tyres are *not* covered by insurance; you won't be charged for a simple puncture, but ruined tyres will have to be paid for. Check the car before you set off, and make sure you've got a spare and a jack (often under the bonnet). Be sure, too, that you understand the terms of the hire contract you have signed (of course this should be available in English). Keep your car hire contract and driving licence with you at all times when out on the road. It's worth taking note of the car hire company's telephone numbers as well, just in case ....

Our car touring notes are brief; they include little information readily available in standard guidebooks — or the handouts you can obtain free from tourist offices at home and tourist information kiosks on the island itself. Instead, we've concentrated on the 'logistics' of touring: times and distances, road conditions, and giving clear directions where you might falter or be misled using other existing maps (the signposting on Crete is not all that it might be). Most of all, we emphasise possibilities for **walking** (if you team up with walkers you may lower your car rental costs) and **picnicking.** The symbol *P* advises you of a picnic spot; see pages 10-12. While some of the suggestions for short walks and picnics may not be suitable during a long car tour, you may find a landscape that you would like to explore at leisure another day.

The large colour touring map is designed to be held out opposite the touring notes and contains all the information you will need outside the towns.* The tours have Hania as their departure/return point, but they could quite easily be joined from other centres. Plans of Hania and Rethimnon, with city exits, are on pages 8 and 9.

*The *reverse* shows walks and tours in *Landscapes of Eastern Crete.*

13

Some points worth noting

We cannot stress too strongly the advantage of taking with you one of the books mentioned on page 6, detailing Crete's history and archaeological heritage. Note also:

- **Allow plenty of time for visits**; the times we give for the tours include only *very* brief stops at viewpoints labelled (☎) in the notes.
- **Telephones** are located at most kiosks, at OTE (telephone exchanges) and in *cafeneions*.
- WC indicates **public toilets**; these are rare, but others are found in restaurants.
- Don't be flummoxed by **Greek road signs**; they are almost invariably followed by English ones.
- You are meant to cross a **solid white line near the edge of the road**, when someone wants to overtake. However, beware of slower vehicles, laden donkeys, bikes, etc ahead, when you round corners.
- Conversely, a **solid white line in the middle of the road** means NO OVERTAKING — regardless of the behaviour of other motorists who appear not to notice it.
- Do think before you pull up to admire a view, if you are not at a **viewpoint** with parking; remember that other motorists cannot see round corners.
- Never throw **cigarette ends** out of the car.
- Come to a standstill at **stop signs**.
- **The spelling of village names** may vary. We haved used the letter 'H' where an 'X' or 'CH' might be used locally; this is to aid pronunciation.
- In towns, only **park your car** where permitted.
- **Priority signs** (red/black/white arrows) on narrow stretches of road give priority to the black arrow.
- You will see shrines in various places (little boxes often carrying a cross and filled with oil, a candle, an icon, pictures, etc). They are a sad warning that sometime in the past a fatal accident involving vehicles has occurred at that spot. **Drive carefully.**

Distances quoted are *cumulative kilometres* from Hania. A key to the symbols in the notes is on the touring map. Note that only the largest churches — or churches that are landmarks — are highlighted, since every village has at least one church! The same can be said of tavernas or *cafeneions*; you should be able to find *some* sustenance almost anywhere en route. **All motorists should read the country code on page 45 and go quietly in the countryside.** *Kalo taxidi!*

1 THE FAR WEST

Hania • (Kasteli) • (Polirinia) • Sfinari • Vathi • Moni
Chrisoskalitisas • (Elafonisi) • Elos • Topolia • Kaloudiana • Hania

*170km/105mi; about 5 hours 15 minutes' driving; Exit B from Hania
(see town plan page 8)*

On route: Picnics (see pages 10-12): (15), 16; Walks 1, 2, (13), (14), (15),
16, 17

*Once off the north coast road, the going is slower, with poor road
surfaces in several areas. The last ten kilometres down to Moni Chrisoskalitisas is very rough and dusty indeed, as is the detour to Elafonisi.
However, all of these roads are being upgraded as of press date.*

You can drive miles through this wild, rugged western
end of Crete and see virtually no-one; on this tour,
you're alone in the landscape. The sea views are dramatic
on the coastal drive and contrast well with the countryside
inland on the return journey. Try to set off early in the
morning, so you have time for a detour to the turquoise
shallows at Elafonisi.

From 1866 Square, take Exit B (Skalidi/Kissamou). This
one-way system is signposted 'Omalos/Kastellion'. There
are plenty of petrol stations along this north coast road, so
fill up (🚇) before turning off. Pass the turning for Omalos
(2km) and continue west. All the beach-side villages on
this route — **Galatas, Kalamaki, Glaros, Kato Stalos** (starting point for Walks 1 and 2 — see photographs on pages
23 and 26), **Agia Marina** (Δ), **Platanias** (where Walk 1 ends)
— have tavernas and rooms and apartments for rent
(🏨🏠Δ✕).

Cross the Keritis River (12km) and drive on (🚇 13.6km),
flanked by orange groves and large patches of bamboo
(🚇 15.5km). Soon the route passes through **Maleme**
(16km 🏨✕🚇). The village saw violent activity during the
Second World War; it was here that the Battle of Crete
flared up. A signpost on the left (17.2km), in German and
Greek, indicates the German war graves.

Continue along the north coast, hemming the sea. You
will see the Rodopou Peninsula (Walks 13 and 14) lunging
out ahead in the middle distance. Drive through **Tavronitis** (19.4km ✕🚇). **Kamisiana** (20.6km ✕) and **Rapaniana**
(21km ✚🏨✕🚇) flash by. On your way through **Skoute-
lonas** (22km), look to the right, at the beginning of the
peninsula, to see Moni Gonia (Walk 14). There is a junction of roads at **Kolimbari** by the Hotel Rosmarie (where
Walk 14 ends). The turning right goes into Kolimbari and
to the Gonia Monastery — see them at leisure another day,
when you can walk down the flower-lined path shown on

page 85. Go straight across at the junction, bending up left and making for Kasteli. Then take a new road that forks off to the right. At press date this road was 3km long, but progressing west. After 1.5km pass a turn to Rodopos, where both Walks 13 (photograph page 81) and 14 start.

Just past **Plakalona** (31km), there is an excellent view straight ahead along the shoreline to Kasteli and over the inland hills. The road leads down through olive trees, past the pretty little church at Lyridiana up left from the road, and bends down towards Kasteli. The dramatic cleft created by the gorge at Roka (**ᵀᵀ**) can be seen now, over to the left. There's a narrow bridge at **Koleni** (35km **☎**) and camping facilities at **Drapanias** (36km Δ; **☎** 37.3km). **Kaloudiana** (39km) is where you would change buses at the end of Walk 16. A kilometre further on, you can look right to the Gramvousa Peninsula (see notes and photograph pages 28-29). You are on the outskirts of Kasteli.

If you wish to make a detour to the site at Polirinia, look out at 40.5km for the turn-off left — it's just beyond the OTE, at a junction with a central triangle, opposite a petrol station (**☎**). There is a small sign up on a wall (in Greek), indicating Polirinia. You'll pass a new church on the left and continue inland, passing another sign for Polirinia at 42km. Drive with care along this potholed asphalt road. Go through Karfiana and Grigoriana before coming to Polirinia ★ (47km **ᵀᵀ✕**). Drive to the end of the road and park near the taverna. Walk 15 ends here; if you'd like to stretch your legs, you could follow some of the walk in reverse, coming to a fine picnic spot in about 20-25 minutes (see notes page 12 and photograph page 86).

The main tour bypasses the Polirinia turn-off and Kasteli ★ (**ᵀᵀ🔺✕☎M**), by continuing on the main road. Kasteli is certainly worth visiting — it has a pleasant atmosphere — but we suggest you come on another day, when you will have time to combine a visit with a walk or even the detour to Polirinia and a swim at Falasarna's beach (mentioned below). Staying on the main road, pass a small harbour and then the Kisamou port. The Gramvousa Peninsula spreads before you directly to the right, a brown-grey mound disappearing into the sea. At 52km a road (rough for the last kilometre) leads down right to Falasarna ★ (**ᵀᵀ**), where there is a good sandy beach — if you feel you have time for a swim. However, it will make your day very long to detour at this stage. If you decide to go for a swim, take the Elafonisi detour later in the day.

So keep up on the main road and head round left into

Platanos, a very strung-out village. Stay on the reasonable asphalt road, watching out for the rough patches. There's a good view back over the beach at 56km (); you can also see the tip of Falasarna. Then pass another good viewpoint at 58km (), over the Bay of Sfinari. In **Sfinari** (62km ✕) we turn away from the sea and head up into the hills. The road passes through the tiny hamlet of **Ano Sfinari** (64km) and winds along beside a ravine, rounding its end at 66km. Beyond **Kambos** (70km) the road is quite rough as it climbs — leaving a steepish drop down to the sea — the next few kilometres to **Keramoti**, a village that juts out on the hillside to the left of the road. Again the road worsens at around 77km. At 78km, keep left; make sure you don't take a track going off to the right. You'll be on

Samaria Gorge: western Crete's most famous walk. Here are the 'Sideroportes' — the 'Iron Gates', where the gorge is at its narrowest, and the rock walls soar up about 600m (2000ft) on either side.

Hania's harbour

asphalt again just before you drive into **Amigdalokefali**, where most of the village is set below the road. **Simadiriana** (81 km) and **Papadiana** (83km) merit another splash of asphalt, as does **Kefali** (85km ✕).

Half a kilometre beyond Kefali, turn right on a very rough road that descends through tree-covered hillsides to **Vathi** (87km). Keep right at Vathi on the rough road to Chrisoskalitisas. Some way past **Plokamiana**, there is a sign to Stomio before a bridge (92km). Disregard this sign and instead cross the bridge (over a riverbed). By 93.5km you can at last see the monastery ahead, with its bright blue roof. A track comes in from the right; turn left round the Bay of Stomio. An ugly rash of houses has sprung up at **Chrisoskalitisas** (95km ✕), just a kilometre from the monastery ★ itself (96km ♣). Having visited the church, you're ready to start the return journey. But first, if you fancy a break and a swim (and if you can put up with another five kilometres of rough road) take the track going off right 0.5km past the monastery. It leads to a lovely sandy beach and turquoise water — protected and created by the nearby Elafonisi Islands; it's a perfect place for a swim.

Retracing the route from Chrisoskalitisas, turn right onto the asphalt road at 107.5km. Past **Louhi** (110km), keep to the main road, curving round to the right at **Limni** (111km) and going into **Elos** (111.5km ✕🍺), a pretty village strung out through chestnut trees. Keep straight on at **Mili** (116km) and look out for any traffic coming in from the right (from Paleohora). Leave **Katsamatados** (Picnic 16; Walks 16 and 17 — see photograph page 91) off to the right at 119.5km. Soon you will have a wonderful view through the Topolia Gorge ★ (120.5km 📷). Just past this obvious viewpoint, there is an old sign at the left of the road indicating the cave chapel of Agia Sophia ★ (♥♣) up on the hillside. Go through the narrow tunnel in the gorge wall — headlights on and hooting. Then continue through the pretty hillside village of **Topolia** (122.5km), where Walk 17 ends. Pass through **Voulgaro** (125.5km 🍺); Walk 16 ends here. Reaching the main coast road at **Kaloudiana** (130km ♣), turn right and head back to Hania.

2 PALEOHORA AND SOUTH COAST BEACHES

**Hania • Tavronitis • Voukolies • Kandanos • Paleohora
Kandanos • (Sougia) • Hania**

152km/94mi; 4 hours' driving; Exit B from Hania (town plan page 8)

On route: Picnics (see pages 10-12): (18); Walks 1, 2, 18

*Driving to Paleohora is very straightforward; once you're on the road,
you really can't go wrong. A major road-widening and improving
programme is underway across the island, and in places it will be
necessary to drive over rough sections of gravel-topped road. The sign
ΠΡΟΣΧΗ ΕΡΓΑ — 'Take care, Works' is a useful one to know.*

You will see two coasts on this trip — the north coast,
which you follow out of Hania, and the south coast at
Paleohora, where there is a long beach stretching for miles
east and west. The route cuts straight across the island
from north to south — climbing up through hillside
villages that saw action during the Second World War —
as far as Kandanos, before descending again through the
district of Selinos — a region rich in Byzantine churches

*Agia's church and lake (Walk 2; Car tour 3). Near the lake is the site of
one of the four major parachute landings made by the German invaders
in 1941. Three battalions of paratroopers landed there, and their task
was to take Hania. The area around Galatas, across the hills from Stalos
(Walks 1 and 2), was the Germans' main point of contact; New Zealand
troops put up fierce resistance there.*

housing a host of frescoes. You might like to make a detour to Anidri, where there is a church of particular interest.

Leave Hania by Exit B, following Car tour 1 as far as **Tavronitis** (19km). Here take the left turn signposted to Paleohora and Kandanos. Pass through **Neranztia** (23.5km; ♔ at 25.5km) and, in **Voukolies** (26km), go through the main square. Head up right, climbing out of this large village and the valley. Wind up through olive trees into the high hills. By about 33km you can see over the sea to the west coast on your right. Then, at **Dromonero** (34km), the countryside opens out, and you enjoy some very fine views. Driving through the spread-out village of **Kakopetros** (38km), follow the road curving round to the right, signposted to Paleohora. Catch your

The deserted village of Myli (Walk 10), accessible from Car tour 8

last glimpse of the north coast — with the Gramvousa Peninsula, shown on pages 28-29, jutting out into the sea. The rockier landscape here is somewhat softened by horse chestnut trees. **Mesavlia** (43.5km) is just a few houses, followed by **Floria** (47km) and **Anavanos**. At the end of the village of **Kandanos** (56km ♣🛒), follow the road round to the right and head south.

Cross a stream at **Plemeniana** (58km; Agios Georgios ♣ with 15th-century frescoes). Further on, more frescoes merit a visit, in **Kakodiki** (63km ♣). Beyond here (at 64km), you can make a short detour left to Agia Tria — just 2km return — to see the frescoed chapel of Mikhail Arkhangelos (♣; the key is with the priest who lives further up the hill). Continuing south, go through **Vlithias** (67km). Soon the sea and the south coast come into view. Pass through **Kalamos** and **Ligia** (72km), and then a rocky valley.

Paleohora (73.5km ▲▲△✖🛒) is approached along an avenue of eucalyptus trees. At 74km, pass the turn-off for Anidri ★, which you might like to visit to see the 14th-century frescoes in Agios Georgios church (♣). If so, take the turn and fork left again at the sea; turn right at the Paleohora Club, then left at a sign 'Camping'. The main tour passes the Anidri turn-off and comes into Paleohora (76km). Turn left just before the road narrows; you can see the clock tower ahead. Park on the sea-side esplanade. Walk 18, from Sougia via the site at Lisos, ends here.

The simplest way to return to Hania is to retrace your outgoing route. However, if you have decided to cover a lot of ground, it's possible to include Sougia in today's tour (add an extra hour). If you opt for this excursion, follow the road back as far as Kandanos (this is really the *best route*, even though some maps indicate roads via Azogires and Anidri). In Kandanos, past the square, take the right turn (signposted to Temenia; opposite the petrol station), which leads south via Anisaraki. In Temenia, pass the turning right (one of the routes from Paleohora — 17km of excruciatingly rough road) and, a kilometre beyond Temenia, at a junction, go left, following signs for Rodovani. Go through Maza, following a rough road through a gorge (📷) down to the sea. You will be back on asphalt when you leave Rodovani. When you meet the main Hania/Sougia road, go right and start heading downhill to the coast. There's a good view of the towering wall of the White Mountains ahead of you as you descend. Drive through Moni and on to Sougia. To return from Sougia, use the notes for Car tour 3, page 24, first paragraph.

3 COUNTRYSIDE, COASTAL BACKWATER AND HIGH CRETAN PASTURELAND

Hania • Nea Roumata • Agia Irini • Epanohori • Sougia • Omalos • Laki • Fournes • Hania

159km/99mi; under 4 hours' driving; Exit B from Hania (plan page 8)

On route: Picnics (see pages 10-12): (3), 18; Walks 2, (3), 18-22

A great deal of country road is involved, which means extra-careful driving and unwavering attention. The section across to Omalos on the return journey is very rough and for adventurous drivers only (but this may be omitted; see page 24). Coming back down from Omalos you are likely to meet coaches — patience and care are required.

This tour takes a very picturesque route through wooded valleys and the Agia Irini Gorge to Sougia, a pleasant backwater. At Sougia, you may like to do the very attractive walk along another gorge to the site at Lisos, and then swim in the lovely clear water from Sougia's pebbly beach, before heading into the hills. If you are not a great walker, but you *are* a good driver, Omalos is a must. So even if you're not going to 'walk Samaria', this tour will take you to the top — where shepherds gather on the plain and eagles and vultures soar overhead.

Fill up with petrol before you leave Hania by Exit B (Skalidi/Kissamou). Turn left at 2km, immediately past the narrow bridge, following signposting for Alikianos and Omalos. Drive through the suburb of **Vamvakopoulo** (🏠)

Here and opposite: the essence of Crete

and then **Agia** (10km), setting for Walk 2. Continue until you see the turning right (12km 🚌) for Alikianos and Skines (opposite a petrol station and a war memorial). Take this right turn and go over the bridge crossing the Keritis River. The road bypasses both Alikianos and Skines. Drive with care and attention on this narrow country road. From **Hilaro** (20km) the old road is being widened, which will help on some of the potentially dangerous bends.

A much-used sign in Crete is one you should keep a watch for: ΠΡΟΣΧΗ ΕΡΓΑ — 'Take care, works'. Soon you are driving through wooded valleys, planted with citrus trees to the left and right. The road starts to climb seriously (22km) and becomes more twisty as it leads through the foothills of the White Mountains. Pass through **Nea Roumata** (29.5km) and **Prases** (30km ✝✗). Glorious hillsides surround you now — covered in chestnut, fig, olive, walnut and plane trees ... to name but a few. Pass by the turn-off for Omalos (38.5km).

Just beyond this turning, the Agia Irini Valley begins on the left; it runs through a gorge and down to the Libyan Sea, emerging at Sougia. Enter **Agia Irini** (42km; 🚌 at 43km, *not open Sundays*). As you leave this village (a sign tells you so at 44km), you pass a track on the left. Twenty minutes' walking along this track leads to some lovely settings among pines (pleasant for a picnic).

Pass through **Epanohori** (45.5km), from where you will have a first glimpse of the Libyan Sea, and start heading down to Sougia — via **Prines**, **Tsiskiana** and **Kambanos** (52km), beyond which the road swings round left and continues through **Maralia** and **Agriles** (56km 🚌, *not on Sundays*). Turn left at the T-junction one kilometre past Agriles (Paleohora is off to the right — 22km of rough road away). In a kilometre or two you will have a splendid view over the valley and down to the sea, tucked neatly into the 'V' ahead. **Moni** is the last village before **Sougia** (67km). Walk 18 sets off from this backwater; see photographs on pages 95 and 99. The setting for Picnic 18, shown on page 99, is only 10-15 minutes from here on foot.

There are some pleasant places to picnic not far below Moni Gouverneto (Car tour 4, Picnic CT4)

The route we describe for the return journey to Hania goes via Omalos and the top of the Samaria Gorge. That sounds very tempting but, unless you are a very experienced driver, it might be better to retrace your outbound route. At present the Omalos road is very rough; parts of it are under construction (don't be fooled by the asphalt at the start).

If you decide to go via Omalos, turn right on the road passed earlier in the day (29km north of Sougia). It soon turns into rough track; stay on the main route, passing a small white church on your right some 9km along, as you go through the pass. Keep right when the track forks by a *cafeneion* sign; by now you will be on the **Omalos**. Keep straight on and, 43km from Sougia, you will reach the main road which leads along the side of the plain to the top of the Samaria Gorge. Then turn right and drive to **Xiloskala** (cover photograph) at the top of the ravine. From here you can look down into the gorge itself (Walk 22; photographs on the cover and pages 17, 108) and up to Gingilos Mountain (Walk 19; photographs on the cover and page 101). You'll also see the route up to the mountain refuge at Kallergi (Walk 20; photograph page 103). We hope this panorama will inspire you to walk!

Alternatively, to return to Hania (an hour's drive away) without visiting Xiloskala, turn left on the main road, on the far side of Omalos, passing the taverna and rooms for rent (🛏🍴) at the edge of the plain. Coach groups stop here for breakfast, en route for Samaria. Leave the plain behind and start to descend towards the distant coast. The most noticeable place on the return route is **Laki** (127km 🛏🍴), a village which overlooks the countryside of Walk 3 (photograph page 50). Take care past here to keep to the road, as it swings round to the right (132km) near the turning to Askordalos. Drive into **Fournes**, go over the bridge and curve left through the village (a right turn leads to Meskla, where Walk 3 ends). Pass the junction to Alikianos, and go straight on (🚌 145km), to meet the main north coast road after 12km. Turn right to Hania.

4 THE AKROTIRI PENINSULA

Hania • Kounoupidiana • Kalathas • Stavros • Agia Triada • Moni Gouverneto • (Souda Bay Cemetery) • Hania

50km/31mi; 1 hour 45 minutes' driving; Exit C from Hania (plan page 8)
On route: Picnic (see pages 10-12): CT4; Walk 12

Except for the access roads to the monasteries and the last stretch of road to Stavros, roads are in good condition. Note: The Gouverneto Monastery is closed from 14.00-17.00, and shorts are not considered proper attire for visiting.

The Akrotiri Peninsula, mushrooming out into the sea northeast of Hania, invites exploration. You may have seen some of it if you flew into Hania's airport, but you won't have seen any of the peninsula's treasures. The ruins of what is purported to be the island's earliest monastery are accessible by foot from this tour — as well as two other monasteries. All three are in lovely, peaceful settings. With splendid views and swimming possibilities, this short car tour could well fill a whole day very pleasantly.

Leave Hania by Exit C: 1.5km from the market, follow the road round to the right, just beyond the Doma Hotel. The road is signposted for Akrotiri and the airport. It climbs up out of Hania, leaving the old part of the town (Halepa) off to the left. The left turn you need to take to get out onto the peninsula is indicated by two signposts (5km): the first is for the Venizelos' Graves and the second for Kounoupidiana. It's an odd junction; take what appears to be the second road left, then go immediately right at the T-junction (signposted 'Kounoupidiana'). But for a wonderful view of Hania, first turn *left* instead of right at this T-junction and drive for two minutes to the Venizelos' Graves, where you can gaze down over the town, the north coast, and Theodorou Island beyond (📷).

Back on the car tour route, very soon after the junction, you will have another splendid view (📷) across Akrotiri to Stavros, where the mountain falls away into the sea. Coming to a fork (7km 🚌), take the right arm, then keep left and start

Stavros, where the mountain falls into the sea and the beach is perfect for swimming and picnicking. 'Zorba the Greek' was filmed here.

25

Stalos church (Walks 1 and 2)

heading downhill, through **Kounoupidiana** (✕).

As you leave the village, turn left at 8km for Stavros. **Kalathas Beach** (9km ✕) is passed, followed by **Horafakia**. About 0.5km beyond the latter, turn left for Stavros. Three kilometres further on, turn right at a junction and come into **Stavros** (✕), where 'Zorba the Greek' was filmed. You might like to picnic by the lovely beach, which is perfect for swimming (see page 25).

Continue the tour by heading back the way you came, as far as the fork in Horafakia (20km). Instead of going right, back to Hania, take the left-hand turning (signposted in Greek: ΑΓ ΤΡΙΑΔΑ). At the next fork (20.5km) keep going round at the sign for Gouverneto, heading towards the mast on the hill ahead. Turn left at the next set of signs (23.7km) — one pointing in the direction you've come from Horafakia, the other the back of the Agia Triada/Gouverneto sign. Drive down the avenue of trees into **Agia Triada** (24km ✝✕).

Having wandered round the monastery ★, head on to Gouverneto, four kilometres away. With your back to Agia Triada, go right and set off on a rough road. A sign for Gouverneto (ΓΟΥΒΕΡΝΕΤΟ) takes you into a right turn at 25km. The road changes from concrete to rough track for the approach to the monastery ★ (**Moni Gouverneto**; 29km ✝). Apart from visiting Gouverneto, why not walk down to the ancient Katholikou Monastery (Walk 12; see photograph page 24). A good rounding-off to your tour.

For the last stage of the excursion, drive back to Agia Triada and, at the junction beyond the monastery (34km), bear left to Hania. A kilometre further on, turn right; the road, signposted to Hania, curves round to the left. Half a kilometre along, turn right and then right again (38km). Where the road divides — at 43km, above Souda Bay — either continue for 7km straight to Hania, or go left and down via the Souda Bay Cemetery and Souda.

Opposite: Fishing boats at Georgioupoli, bringing in their catch for all the local restaurants. Early morning is a good time to catch them. (Car tour 6; Walks 7 and 8).

5 THE FOOTHILLS OF THE LEVKA ORI (THE WHITE MOUNTAINS)

Hania • Aptera • Katohori • Kambi • Mournies • Hania

67km/42mi; 2 hours' driving; Exit A from Hania (town plan page 8)
On route: Picnics (see pages 10-12): 5a, 5b, 6; Walks (4), 5, 6
On the whole, the roads are reasonable to good. The section from Katohori to Kambi, where there are occasional potholes, needs care.

History and hills combine nicely on this tour, which is a short spin into the lovely countryside inland from Hania. With the wild flowers of spring, the stillness of high summer or the colours of autumn, it's a pleasant morning or afternoon circuit. You'll drive to the fringe of the Levka Ori — often snow-capped until mid-summer.

Leave Hania by Exit A (Apokoronou). At the end of this tree-lined avenue (🚌) leading away from the town, follow the road round to the right (Souda is straight on) and, moments later, turn left onto the main highway, sign-

posted to Rethimnon. Make the first move off the beaten track by turning right for Aptera at 12km. At the junction in **Megala Horafia** (13km), turn hard left; after one kilometre, you will see **Aptera★** (**Π**; roadside parking) spread out to the right. Drive on to the Turkish fort perched up in a commanding position over Souda Bay (15km ⚐).

From the fort go back to the junction in Megala Horafia and turn sharp left for Stilos, heading down through undulating hills. Make another sharp turn, this time to the right, at 20km. Beyond **Malaxa,** at 29km, turn left for Kontopoula, signposted in Greek (Κοντοπουλα). (Turning *right* at this point, you would find a good taverna with magnificent views, a minute away, ✗⚐.) Head on to **Kontopoula** (32km) — a gorgeous panorama of hills and mountains is ahead of you. The next collection of houses on the route is **Katohori** (34km). At the far end of this village, turn left over the bridge. Walk 5 starts here, and some 5-15 minutes' walking would take you to the views shown on pages 55 and 56 — both lovely picnic spots (Picnics 5a and 5b). Make for **Kambi** (Καμπι; 38km) and take the right-hand fork into the village square. The church is on the right; there is a pleasant *cafeneion* just beyond it. Walk 6 starts here. A ten-minute excursion on foot would take you to a setting similar to that shown on page 60 (Picnic 6).

Return the way you came; after the bridge at Katohori turn left instead of right. At the junction in **Gerolakos** (47km) turn right (a left turn leads to Drakonas; Walk 4; photograph page 53). Past **Loulos**, **Aletrouvari** and **Panagia** (where you pass a war memorial on the left), the route curves down the side of a steep valley, through **Vantes** and into **Mournies** (62km). At 64km turn left and go straight over at the next crossroads (66km). Straight over again at the next lights — and soon come to Hania's market.

6 A SLICE OF CRETE

Hania • Vrises • Askyfou • Hora Sfakion • Frango-kastello • Selia • Moni Preveli • Rethimnon • Episkopi • Georgioupoli • Hania

240km/149mi (via the old road from Rethimnon); 223km/138mi (via the new road from Rethimnon); 6-7 hours' driving; Exit A from Hania (town plan page 8)

On route: Picnics (see pages 10-12): 8, 25, CT6; Walks 7, 8, 25, 26, 27. (Walks 23 and 24 are nearby.)

The road south — from the moment it starts to climb up and over the foothills of the White Mountains, until it reaches the coast at Hora Sfakion — is a mass of tortuous loops ... and the driver had better have a head for heights. There are a lot of well-driven buses and coaches on this road — but keep in and keep hooting!

You'll sample a bit of everything on this tour, which encompasses a neat square of the island. First we head south, following the same route thousands of retreating, war-weary Antipodean and British soldiers trudged over during World War II. We call in at the pretty harbour village of Hora Sfakion, from where boats ply west to Loutro, Agia Roumeli at the foot of the Samaria Gorge, and Paleohora. We turn east, following the coast to Frango-kastello, a solitary landmark, once a fortified castle. Past the Kotsifas Gorge, we visit one of Crete's most beautiful monasteries, Moni Preveli, set in glorious solitude. Heading north, we leave the views over the Libyan Sea, following the Kourtaliotis Gorge to Rethimnon. Here it's really worth getting out of the car to walk down to a magical spot where there is a waterfall and a small church tucked away. From there it's back to base — either via the old country road or, more directly, along the new main highway.

Take Exit A out of Hania (Apokoronou), heading east on the main coast road and leaving Souda down to the left.

A mesmerising turquoise lagoon, fringed with bleached white sand, and one of the islands off the shore at Gramvousa. A good track now extends almost to the end of the peninsula. From the end of the track you could follow a path to the far northwest corner of Crete and enjoy a swim. There's no shade, so do remember to take a sunhat! Gramvousa is easily reached from Car tour 1.

Pass the turning off to Aptera ★ (12km; Car tour 5). At 30km, be sure not to miss the turning right to Vrises: it is almost immediately after you come under a bridge — where there's an old blue sign in English and Greek at the junction. Turn left at the junction immediately afterwards (31km), and enter the outskirts of **Vrises**. Go straight through the village (33km), over the bridge, and continue straight on (disregard the left turn to Rethimnon). You will be heading south, with the magnificent White Mountains lying to the right. Pass the turning left to Alikampos at 37km. Walk 8 starts there (photograph page 66).

The road twists uphill, and the landscape becomes rockier and greyer with the climb. There's a splendid sight as you round a corner (47km 📷): the plain of Askyfou, shown on pages 122-123, spreads out across to the left of the road. A striking Turkish fort sits on a mound in the foreground. **Kares** (48km) is the little village on the hillock down to the left; Walk 26 starts here. The road hems the plain, and the next village is the main one of the area, **Askyfou** itself (49km 🍴). Drive on round the plain and then follow the road as it heads south again. This is the route that thousands of soldiers from Britain, Australia and New Zealand took when fleeing western Crete.

The road skirts the Imbros Gorge, which you see down left at 55km. Walk 25 starts here; a twenty-minute walk from **Imbros** would take you to the setting for Picnic 25 — see photograph on page 118. Shortly (at 59km), if you look left again, you can see along the south coast to the east — including Frangokastello. But you are still high up above

As you travel towards Prasies (Car tour 8), you see Vrissinas, the highest peak across the valley. This photograph was taken from Vrissinas, where there is a Minoan sanctuary (Walk 11). Jerusalem sage lines the path.

The sea and beach at Plakias, seen from just one of the many good outlooks along the route of Walk 27 and Car tour 6.

the sea for the time being; you still have to drive carefully as the road snakes its way down to the coast in tortuous loops. At 68km, the coast road comes in from the east. Continue down and on into the pretty village shown on page 119, **Hora Sfakion ★** (72km 📷 ✕). As you curve down into the village, take the lower road to the harbour. Walks 22-25 finish at Hora Sfakion — by boat or on foot.

Head back out the way you came in and reach a fork at 75km. Follow signs for Patsianos, carrying straight on along the coast. Pass through **Komitades** (76km); Walk 25 — which started out at Imbros — can end here at Komitades, or at Hora Sfakion. Continue on through **Vraskas**, **Vouvas**, **Nomikiana** and **Agios Nektarios** (where Walk 26 ends); then turn right at 83km for Frangokastello, heading down towards the sea. Four kilometres of rough road carry you to **Frangokastello ★** (87km 🏛). After wandering round the ruined castle, carry on along the same coast road, still heading east. Turn right at the junction (90km), where there is a signpost for **Skaloti**. Drive through that village and on to **Argoules**. Cross a stream and come into **Ano Rodakino** and **Kato Rodakino** (100km).

Beyond the right-hand turn to Koraka Beach, the views are well worth stopping to admire. There is a particularly good viewpoint looking back west along the coast at 103km, and you can park at 104km to admire the panorama (📷): steep cliffs plunge down to the sea on your right, and the inland landscape is dramatically rocky and barren. A few kilometres further on you have wonderful views in all directions, with the peaks of hills jutting up all round … but nowhere to park the car.

The road bends down through **Selia** (111km). At 112km, take the sharp right-hand turn downhill (the road from Rethimnon, which follows the Kotsifas Gorge). From **Mirthios** (114km 📷✕) there is a fine view over Plakias. Turn left at the junction (115km), where a sign indicates 'Plakias 3km right'. (But turn right if you wish to go to Plakias Beach — for a swim or a taverna lunch. Walk 27, shown in the photograph above, is based on Plakias.)

Agia Galini (Car tour 7) is a very popular tourist destination, so try to visit out of season. From this charming port there are views north to the Ida Range (Psiloritis).

Then pass **Mariou,** set well up away from the sea; flat, cultivated land is on your right.

If you decide not to visit the Preveli Monastery (which would be a great pity), you will find Rethimnon signposted at **Asomatos** (122km 🚌).

Here the main tour turns down sharp right into a bend; you will be heading almost back on yourself (there is a signpost here for the monastery and Lefkogia). After 123km turn left onto tarmac road and follow it all the way to the monastery. To the left you see the Kourtaliotis Gorge. Pass the ruins of the original 16th-century monastery ★ and keep on the road. Soon, just round a corner, over the hill, **Moni Preveli ★** (129km ⚓) comes into view. The setting is beautiful and very peaceful. The monastery is open from 08.00-13.00 and from 15.00 to 18.00; shorts are *not* considered suitable attire, if you plan to visit.

The tour continues from Preveli by retracing the route, past the original monastery and back to the bridge, where you turn right (133km) and rejoin the main road (135km). In Asomatos again, turn right (136km), following signs to Rethimnon. This route takes us along the Kourtaliotis Gorge for a short way. Look out for railings and small signs; just before them, there is a place to park on the right. Do make the effort to walk down — and up — here. If you're lucky there won't be a coachload of other visitors. The path leads to a well-placed church and a splashing cool waterfall (Picnic CT6).

From here we head north. The countryside opens out at **Koxare** (143km) and, when we meet the main Rethimnon/Agia Galini road (144km), we turn left (🚌 151km). Pass a turning left to Hora Sfakion and continue into **Armeni** (157km 🚌). Before long the sea and the north coast are in sight in the distance and, as you approach Rethimnon, there is a very good view over the town and the new harbour (📻). Follow the road round, first to the left and then to the right, heading for the town centre. At the traffic lights (167km), turn left for Hania — or else park and explore **Rethimnon ★ (𝐢𝐓🔺✕🍷⊕M)**. The old harbour is a good place to stretch your legs. More than any other town on Crete, this still speaks of its medieval past, with its Ottoman and Venetian buildings. The museum houses a collection of coins and antiquities.

Leaving Rethimnon, either stay on the main highway or, if you've still got some energy, follow us: look for the signpost two kilometres out of town indicating the old road to Hania and take the left turning a kilometre beyond it (171km). Immediately you will drive through **Gerani**, then **Askipopoulo**, **Prines**, **Gonia** and **Agios Andreas** — in quick succession. They are country villages set along a wooded valley. **Episkopi** (189km 🍷) is rather larger. Just past the turning to Φιλακι (Filaki), look straight ahead, and you will see a low dip, with mountains receding behind it. Walk 8 (see photograph page 66) brings you down there on your descent from Alikampos to Kournas.

Go left (193km) towards Kournas, turning onto a dirt road that heads inland. Keep straight on when Filaki is indicated left again. There is a pretty church at the beginning of **Kournas** village (196km ✝📻). Climb up through the village square, leaving a new church on your right. As you leave Kournas, you will see the north coast again, and then Crete's only freshwater lake will come into view below — a lovely, invigorating sight (198km; Picnic 8).

Pass the end of the lake and follow signs to Hania, passing the end of Walk 8 at 201 km. Turn left for Hania at the junction (203km) and cross over the main east/west national road to come into the main square of **Georgiou-poli** (204km 🔺🔺✕). Walk 7 makes a pleasing circuit from this village to Selia and back (photographs page 27 and 63). Turn left in front of the kiosk and go down an avenue of eucalyptus trees. The main road runs along to the left of this country road. Turn left at 210km to join the main road (there is no signposting, but there is a solitary building on the right). Turn right for Hania. Pass the Venetian fort that is now a prison known by its Turkish name, Itzedin, and continue to Hania.

It's much easier to get into the centre of town if you leave the national road where Souda is indicated right (*not* the ferry terminal, which comes up first) — then turn left at the junction and go back to town the way you came out.

7 CRETAN TREASURES

Hania • (Rethimnon) • Armeni • Spili • Agia Galini • Festos • Agia Triada • Hania

264km/164mi; about 6 hours' driving; Exit A from Hania (see town plan page 8)

On route: no walks or picnics

This route follows major roads all the way. But never assume there won't be any potholes; subsidence on the southbound stretch has left damage you will have to reckon with when driving.

Well, this *is* a long haul, but it takes in a very large slice of Cretan landscape on the way to its goals, Festos and Agia Triada. We've included it in the book because we are sure that many of you will want to make the effort to see two of Crete's major sites, even though you are based in western Crete. To reach our destination, we travel via Spili — an exceedingly picturesque spot — and then between Mt Kedros and Siderotas. Agia Galini is included in the itinerary, since you will no doubt have heard of it, and you may wish to see this bustling seaside resort ... needless to say, it is packed with tourists in the summer.

Leave Hania by Exit A (Apokoronou). At the end of the tree-lined avenue (⛽) leading away from the town, follow the road round to the right at 6km (Souda will be signposted straight on). Moments later, turn left onto the main highway, signposted for Rethimnon. Pass the turnings for Aptera★ (Car tour 5), Vrises and Hora Sfakion (30km; Tour 6), and Georgioupoli (33km; also Tour 6). The road we're on is known as the 'new road', and it runs directly along by the sea from Georgioupoli to Rethimnon (⛽ at 41 km; ✕⛽ at 48km). You will have a good view of Rethimnon from the outskirts and then pass the turn-off left to the Old Harbour at 59km. Keep straight on for the centre of town. Soon, at the first set of traffic lights, turn right for Agia Galini.

Head south now, passing through **Armeni** (70km ⛽ and nearby Minoan cemetery Π★), **Mixorouma** (86km ⛽) and **Spili** (89km ▲▲✕), a large and pretty village well worth a 'pit stop'. Continue via **Kisou Kampos** (95km ⛽), and watch out for road subsidence around **Akoumia** (98km), where the road doubles back on itself briefly. Look up to the top of Psiloritis — which is quite likely to be snow-capped until high summer. Take a moment, too, to admire the whole Ida range (📷), with Mt Kedros in the foreground.

Take the turning to **Agia Galini** at 112km. The road

divides: go left and drive down to the harbour of this busy resort (114km ▲▲✕🅿). Having stretched your legs by the harbour — where you can capture some picture-postcard scenes like the one on page 32 — head back to the main road. Turn right at the junction, following the road (△✕ at 116km) signposted to Iraklion. At 122km you drive into the county of Iraklion, past a mass of plastic greenhouses, and then on via the ugly, functional spread of **Timbaki** (127km 🅿). Before long you will see a sign in Greek and then a sign in English indicating that Festos is 2km ahead and Agia Triada 5km.

When you reach the goal of today's pilgrimage, **Festos ★** (129km **Π**✕ WC), make the most of the facilities and information available at the tourist pavilion to appreciate this Minoan site. The setting is glorious — with views towards the Dikti and Lasithi mountains to the east, the Ida range to the north, and the Asterousias to the south. From Festos, carry on through the car park and fork right. This turning takes you back towards the Mesara Plain, to a spot from which you can walk down to **Agia Triada ★** (132km **Π**) in a few minutes. The remains of this Minoan summer palace are also in a delightful setting.

When it's time to head for home, simply retrace the route back to Hania. If you feel energetic enough to make a detour, why not try the 'old road' from Rethimnon to Hania — this route is described on page 33, beginning in the second paragraph.

Crocus

8 THE AMARI VALLEY

Hania • Rethimnon • Apostoli • Thronos • Fourfouras • Agios Ioannis • Gerakari • Rethimnon • Hania

240km/149mi; 6 hours' driving; Exit A from Hania (see plan page 8)

On route: Picnics (see pages 10-12): (10a, 10b), CT8; Walks 9, (10, 11), 28

The tour follows predominantly reasonable asphalted country roads, but they are narrow in places.

The Amari Valley forms a natural route from the north to the south and so was much used as a refuge during the Second World War. Encircled by some forty villages and dotted with Byzantine churches, the valley offers up lovely countryside along our immediate route. But we also enjoy awe-inspiring, sweeping views encompassing the southwest slopes of Psiloritis, Crete's highest peak, and the string of mountains formed by Kedros, Soros, Fortetza and Vrissinas.

Follow the notes for Car tour 7 (page 34), to the first set of traffic lights in Rethimnon (59.5km). Go straight over at the lights (where a left turn would take you into the town centre and a right turn is signposted for Agia Galini). Come to a second set of lights (where there is a statue of Venizelous on the right) and go straight over. Cross straight over again at the third set of lights. Then, if you *do* want to stop in **Rethimnon ★** (**⊓ ▲ ✕ 🍴⊕M**), turn left at 60km and drive to the town beach, where you can easily park. Walks 10 and 11, and Picnics 10a and 10b are easily reached from Rethimnon.

Continuing straight ahead on the main road, you will drive through Perivolia, a suburb of Rethimnon, where Walk 10 can end. Here there's a sign (62km) to Amari and Iraklion (but it's placed too high up to be seen easily, so look out for it). Past this sign, the road forks either side of a Mamadakis petrol station (63km 🍴). *Don't* curve round slightly left with the road; instead, take the right-hand fork, which is *not* signposted. Keep straight on, disregarding the turning left for the 'new road' to Iraklion. You are heading towards Amari. The road climbs gradually into the hills, away from Rethimnon and the coast. As you travel towards Prasies, looking southwest, you will see Vrissinas (858m) — the highest peak across the valley and the goal of Walk 11. **Prasies** (71km ♣) is very pretty and shows signs of its Venetian past. Beyond the village, at the top of a ridge (72km), you enjoy the spectacular panorama towards the Prassanos Gorge shown on page 69 (📷). Soon, just past the turning right to Mirthios, you pass the starting point for Walk 9, which takes you into this gorge.

Take care at a narrow bridge (74km), which has to be negotiated before you descend into the valley (80km ✕🍴). Then the road climbs up again, out of the valley, and runs along beside it. **Apostoli** (90km ♣✕ and 🍴 just beyond the village) is at the head of the Amari Valley. Our circuit will bring you back to this point. Keep straight on through **Agia Fotini** (91 km 🍴) and stay on the main road until, on a bend, you see a sign for **Thronos.** It leads you left and up to the village (92km ♣). After visiting the church, return to the main road and turn left, continuing the circuit. Pass below Kalogeros (♣ with 14th-century frescoes), a pretty hillside village set up to the left of the road, and — a minute beyond here — look right to see the small 15th-century Byzantine church of Agia Paraskevi.

Pass the junction (93.5km) to Amari and keep straight on the main road (🚉 97km) as it curves left. Go through **Afratas** (100km) and continue through groves of ancient olive trees. The views are good all around — particularly when you look right towards Amari. Then come into **Visari** (103km). The road curls round the edge of the village and heads up to **Fourfouras** (105km 🚉). Walk 28 (see photograph on page 128) starts in this village, which is mainly set down to the right of the road. Behind Fourfouras lies Mt Kedros (1777m) — a very comfortable mound, compared to the tantalising jagged teeth and high slopes of Psiloritis to the left of the road. Two kilometres past Fourfouras, as you continue to climb, look right and back over the village and the entire basin of the Amari Valley below you (📷).

Drive on via **Kouroutes** (112km 🏃) and **Nithavris** (116km). Here, at the end of the village, turn right (by a war memorial) to Agios Ioannis. This route cuts across the valley and goes through the upper part of **Agios Ioannis** (120km). Turn sharp right at 120.5km for Rethimnon; don't mistake this turn and head for Agia Paraskevi. The turning for Rethimnon now takes you through the lower part of Agios Ioannis.

As you cross a bridge (125.5km) over the River Platys look over to the right to see the very picturesque old bridge shown on page 72 — the setting for Picnic CT8. Past the bridge, the road starts to climb up the west side of the valley, above the olive tree line. We go through **Hordaki** (132km) in a matter of moments and **Ano Meros** (136km) — a somewhat tumbled-down, but not unattractive village of red-roofed houses. There's a striking war memorial at the far end of the village, portraying a woman with a hammer in her hand. To the right of the small village of **Drigies** (138km) rises Mt Samitos. Move on through **Vrises** and **Kardaki** to **Gerakari** (145km), which is visibly greener — even in autumn — than the countryside through which we have taken you. A cemetery on the left precedes **Meronas** (150km 🏃), where fresh mountain water pours down hillsides.

Agia Fotini (155km) comes up next. Turn left here, following signposting to Rethimnon. Go straight into Apostoli. We have now completed the Amari Valley circuit and in forty minutes you will be back in Rethimnon. Once past the turning for the 'new road' to Iraklion, turn left past the Mamadakis petrol station (181km 🚉) and drive back through the town and on to Hania.

❀ Walking

Western Crete is certainly a walkers' paradise but, even if you aren't an avid walker, there are plenty of opportunities for gentle strolls and rambles in the depths of the countryside, where you will develop a real appreciation for this magnificent corner of Greece. So if you can't 'do Samaria', you *could* manage a good number of our walks in western Crete. And one of the best features of these other walks is that from start to finish you will be alone with the landscape and a few local people ... bliss.

The 'Landscapes' series is built around walks and excursions that can be done in day trips from your base. However, if it suits you, it is possible to link a certain number of our western Crete walks by spending a night or two away from your hotel — thus making a patchwork of mountain, gorge and coastal paths (see Walks 19-24).

There are, of course, many more walks in western Crete than those we have described in this book, but most of them would involve being based in a more out-of-the-way location — or they would be quite far off a bus route. We feel that the walks we have included present an attractive cross-section of land and seascapes — the real character of western Crete.

Some words of advice: **Never try to get from one walk to another on uncharted terrain.** Only link up walks by following paths described in these notes, or by using roads or tracks. Don't try to cross rough country, unless you are in the company of a local guide — it might be dangerous. **Never** try to cross military installations or to take photographs in the area.

Do greet anyone you pass or see working in a field when you are out walking. The people you meet are very much a part of the landscape, countryside and essence of Crete, and will reciprocate your gesture of friendliness and acknowledgement.

There are walks in this book for everyone:

Beginners: Start on the walks graded 'easy' or 'straight-forward'; good examples are Walks 1, 2, 3, 4, 7, 14, 17, 20 and 25. *You need look no further than the picnic suggestions on pages 10-12 to find a large selection of very easy walks.*

Experienced walkers: If you are accustomed to rough

terrain and are feeling fit, you should be able to manage and enjoy all the walks in this book. Several of them are very long, so your hiking experience will stand you in good stead. Note that a couple of walks will demand that you have a head for heights. Take into account the season and weather conditions. Don't attempt the more strenuous walks in high summer; do protect yourself from the sun and carry ample water and fruit. *Always remember that storm damage could make any walk described in this book unsafe.* Remember, too, always to follow the route as we describe it. If you have not come to one of our landmarks after a reasonable time, you *must* go back to the last 'sure' point and start again.

Experts: Head for the high mountains. Both the White Mountains and the Ida Range (Psiloritis) will be a great attraction for you (Walks 6,19, 21, 22, 28).

Guides, waymarking, maps

Experienced walkers, used to taking compass readings, will not need a guide for any walk in this book, but should you wish to go further afield we suggest you contact the Greek Alpine Club (EOS), beneath Olympic Airways on Tsanakaki in Hania, or the refuge at Kallergi (above Omalos). The refuge is under the management of Josef Schwemberger, an Austrian, who speaks English. The refuge has a telephone; ask a local agent or your representative to find out the number, which is allocated annually. (Likourgos Dimotakis, at Aptera Travel, 11 V. Ktistaki Street, Hania, will know it.)

Many of the routes in the west of the island are **waymarked**, some by daubs of red paint, some by cairns.

You cannot purchase large-scale **maps** of Greece, for military reasons. Do *not* try to obtain any from the local authorities on Crete; at the very least, you will be viewed with suspicion. We've drawn up our routes in the field and superimposed them on Greek maps dating from the 1930s. Bear in mind that, since we had *no* up-to-date maps for reference, it was virtually *impossible* to make our routes *exact*. Remember, too, that while some tracks and paths shown on these maps are unlikely to exist today, so many new tracks are being built, that our sketch maps are often out of date within weeks. For this reason we have *not* included new tracks on these maps; instead, we give time checks along the route. The notes themselves should enable you to do any walk without problems; we hope the maps will give you a feel for the 'lie of the land'.

Things that bite or sting

Dogs on Crete, in our experience, are full of bravado, but not vicious. They bark like fury — indeed, what would be the point of guarding livestock if they did not? — and they will approach you, seemingly full of evil intention. However, they will shy off, if you continue unperturbed. 'El-la' is a useful word to know. It means 'come here', if spoken encouragingly, or 'come off it', when said in a slightly diffident tone. Use it encouragingly with the dogs, and they'll soon calm down. If you carry a walking stick, keep it out of sight and don't use it threateningly.

In the autumn you may be startled by **gunfire**, but it's only hunters — invariably on Sundays and holidays — in pursuit of game. You'll doubtless see them dropping or throwing stones into bushes — Greek beating!

Have respect for **donkeys'** hind legs; it's highly unlikely they'll kick, but don't forget the possibility.

Snakes may be seen, and **vipers** have been identified on Crete, but they keep a very low profile. Poisonous **spiders**, called 'rogalida', do exist on the island, but it's unlikely you'll glimpse one of these burrowers. You're more likely to see **scorpions**; they are harmless, but their sting is painful. They, like spiders and snakes, are most likely hiding under rocks and logs in the daytime. So if you move a rock etc to sit down, just have a look under it first!

People who are allergic to bee stings should always carry the necessary pills with them. **Bees** abound in high summer, especially around water troughs and thyme bushes. It's also worth taking a plug-in **mosquito** deterrent, mosquito repellent, and some anti-sting ointment.

What to take

If you're already on Crete when you find this book, and you haven't any special equipment such as a rucksack or walking boots, you can still do many of the walks — or you can buy the basic equipment. For each walk in the book, the *minimum* equipment is listed. But it would be a good idea to consider this checklist before setting out:

stout shoes with ankle support or walking boots; (long) socks	sunhat, sunglasses, suncream
	spare bootlaces
waterproof rain gear (outside summer months)	insect repellent, antiseptic cream
	up-to-date bus timetable
long-sleeved shirt (sun protection)	bandages, plasters, tissues
long trousers, tight at the ankles	knives and openers
water bottle, plastic plates, etc	light cardigans (or similar)
anorak (zip opening)	small rucksack
whistle, torch, compass	plastic groundsheet

Please bear in mind that we've not done *every* walk in this book under *all* conditions. We do know that you need plenty of water for every walk, but we might not realise, for example, just how hot or how exposed some walks might be. Beware the sun and the effects of dehydration. Don't be deceived by cloud cover: you can still get sunburnt, especially on the back of your neck and legs. *Always* carry a long-sleeved shirt and long trousers to put on when you've had enough sun, and **always wear a sunhat.** Have your lunch in a shady spot on hot days and carry a good supply of water and fruit. In spring and autumn, remember that it might be quite chilly in the mountains. We rely on your good judgement to modify the 'equipment' list at the start of each walk, according to the season.

W here to stay

We have used Hania as our walking base, since the majority of people stay there when visiting western Crete. But we have taken into account those of you staying at Rethimnon, Kasteli, or along the south coast, and you will find that you can join many of the car tours without difficulty. If you wish to do some of the walks, several will be on your doorstep, but check in the bus timetables (pages 131-132) to make sure that the walks furthest from your base are practicable. Due to the size of the island, some of the walks in the west require bus changes. Although this makes the day longer, it has the advantage that you see more of the countryside. To find rooms in small villages, enquire at the local tavernas and *cafeneions* about renting a bed for a night. An overnight stay at Kallergi is recommended for those of you tackling the Levka Ori (see page 39, 'Guides').

W eather

April, May, September and October are perhaps the best months to walk on Crete. The air temperature is moderate, but the sun shines. It *is* possible to walk during June, July and August, however, because although it may be very hot by the coast, there's often a light breeze in the mountains. There's no doubt it's more tiring though, and great care should be taken in the sun and heat. Walks offering no shade at all (for instance Walk 13 on the Rodopou Peninsula) should *never* be undertaken in high summer.

The *meltemi* blowing in from the north tends to be a bad-tempered wind, bringing strong hot breezes in the height of summer. These breezes stir up the dust, move the air about, but don't really cool it.

During February and November it often rains. The months of December and January are chilly and, if it rains, it may do so for two or three days at a time. However, the winter in Crete brings an incredible clarity on the clear sunny days and some really perfect walking weather, when temperatures may be around 20°C (68°F).

It's worth remarking too that, more often than not, when it's windy along the north coast, it's invariably calm on the south of the island.

Walkers' checklist
The following points cannot be stressed too often:

- **At any time a walk may become unsafe** due to storm damage or road construction. If the route is not as described in this book, and your way ahead is not secure, do *not* attempt to continue.
- **Never walk alone** — four is the best walking group.
- **Do not overestimate your energies**: your speed will be determined by the slowest walker in the group.
- **Transport connections** at the end of a walk are vital.
- **Proper footwear** is essential.
- **Warm clothing** is needed in the mountains; even in summer, take something appropriate with you, in case you are delayed.
- **Compass, torch, whistle** weigh little, but might save your life.
- **Extra food** and drink should be taken on long walks.
- **Always take a sunhat** with you, and in summer a cover-up for your arms and legs as well.
- A **stout stick** is a help on rough terrain.
- **Do not panic** in an emergency.
- Read and re-read the **important note on page 2** and the country code on page 45, as well as guidelines on grade and equipment for each walk you plan to do.

Greek for walkers
In the major tourist centres you hardly need to know any Greek but, once out in the countryside, a few words of the language will be helpful ... and much appreciated.

Here's one way to ask directions in Greek *and understand the answers you get!* First memorise the 'key' questions below. Then, always follow up your key question with a **second question demanding a yes (*ne*) or no (*ochi*) answer.** Greeks invariably raise their heads to say 'no', which looks to us like the beginning of a 'yes'. (By the way, 'ochi' (no) might be pronounced as **o**-hee, **o**-shee or even **oi**-ee.)

Following are the two most likely situations in which you may have to use some Greek. The dots (...) show where you fill in the name of your destination. See Index for the approximate pronunciation of place names.*

■ **Asking the way**

The key questions

English	Approximate Greek pronunciation
Good day, greetings	**Hair**-i-tay
Hello, hi (informal)	**Yas**-sas (plural); **Yia**-soo (singular)
Please — where is	**Sas** pa-ra-ka-**loh**— **pou ee**-nay
the road that goes to ... ?	o **thro**-mo stoh ... ?
the footpath that goes to ... ?	ee mono-**pati** stoh ... ?
the bus stop?	ee **sta**-ssis?
Many thanks.	Eff-hah-ree-**stoh** po-li.

Secondary question leading to a yes/no answer

English	Approximate Greek pronunciation
Is it here?/there?	**Ee**-nay etho?/eh-**kee**?
Is it straight ahead?/behind?	**Ee**-nay kat-eff-**thia**?/pee-**so**?
Is it to the right?/left?	**Ee**-nay thex-**ya**?/aris-teh-**rah**?
Is it above?/below?	**Ee**-nay eh-**pano**?/**kah**-to?

■ **Asking a taxi driver to take you somewhere and return for you, or asking a taxi driver to collect you somewhere**

English	Approximate Greek pronunciation
Please —	**Sas** pa-ra-ka-**loh**—
Would you take us to ...?	Tha **pah**-reh mas stoh ...?
Come and pick us up	**El**-la na mas **pah**-reh-teh
from ... (place) at ... (time)	apo ... stees ...

(Instead of memorising the hours of the day, simply point out on your watch the time you wish to be collected.)

As you may well need a taxi for some walks, why not ask your tour rep or hotel reception to find a driver who speaks English. We'd also recommend that you use an inexpensive phrase book: they give easily-understood pronunciation hints, as well as a good selection of useful phrases. It's unlikely that a map will mean anything to the people you may meet en route. Doubtless, they will ask you, '**Pooh pah**-tay'? — at the same time turning a hand over in the air, questioningly. It means 'Where are you going?', and quite a good answer is 'Stah voo-**na**', which means 'To the mountains'. (We could insert here a long list of their comments on this, to which you would smile and plough on, 'Landscapes' guide in hand ... .)

*Accents are not printed on place names in the text, lest it slow up your reading, however they *are* shown in the Index and on the maps.

Organisation of the walks

The twenty-eight main walks in this book are located in the parts of western Crete most easily accessible by public transport, using Hania as the base. We hope that even if you are staying at another location in the west, most will be within range. (Although the walking notes show bus departures from Hania, you will find more complete timetables on pages 131-132, including Rethimnon, Kasteli, etc.)

The book is set out so that you can plan walks easily — depending on how far you want to go, your abilities and equipment — and what time you are willing to get up in the morning! You might begin by considering the fold-out touring map between pages 14 and 15. Here you can see at a glance the overall terrain, the road network, and the location of all the walks, which are outlined in white. Quickly flipping through the book, you'll find that there's at least one photograph for each walk.

Having selected one or two potential excursions from the map and the photographs, look over the planning information at the beginning of each walk description. Here you'll find distance/hours, grade, equipment, and how to get there and return. If the walk sounds beyond your ability or fitness, check if there's a shorter or alternative version given. We've tried to provide walking opportunities less demanding of agility wherever possible.

When you are on your walk, you will find that the text begins with an introduction to the overall landscape and then quickly turns to a detailed description of the route itself. Times are given for reaching certain points in the walk. Giving times is always tricky, because they depend on so many factors, but once you've done one walk you'll be able to compare our very steady pace with your own; we hope you'll find we're in step, give or take! Note that our times *do not include any stops*, so allow for them.

The large-scale maps (see notes on page 39: 'Guides, waymarking, maps') have been overprinted to show key landmarks and walking times. Below is a key:

<u>RED</u> main (red) road on the touring map	walking times 1h10' (1 hour; 10 minutes)	• water source, ▼ tank, etc
<u>YELLOW</u> secondary (white) road on touring map	✝ church, etc	⁰ cave
<u>BROWN</u> track (in outline on the touring map	⚜ shrine	🚗 car parking
GREEN→ route of the walk	✳ windmill	🚌 bus stop
GREEN→ alternative walk	○ winnowing circle	Π site, ruins
		👁 best views
		P picnic spot

A country code for walkers and motorists

Observance of certain unwritten rules is essential when out walking or driving in the countryside anywhere, but particularly on Crete's rugged terrain, where irresponsible behaviour can lead to dangerous mistakes. Whether you are an experienced rambler or not, it is important to adhere to a country code, to avoid causing damage, harming animals, or even endangering your own life.

Iris cretica

- **Do not take risks.** Do not attempt walks beyond your capacity, and do not wander off the paths described if there is any sign of enveloping cloud or if it is late in the day.
- **Do not walk alone** and *always* tell someone exactly where you are going and what time you plan to return. On any but a very short walk near to villages, be sure to take a compass, whistle, torch, extra water and warm clothing, as well as some high energy food, like chocolate. This may sound 'over the top' to an inexperienced walker, but it could save your life.
- **Do not light fires**; everything gets tinder dry. If you smoke, make absolutely sure cigarettes are completely extinguished.
- **Do not frighten animals.** The goats and sheep you may encounter are not used to strangers. By making a noise, trying to touch or photograph them, you may cause them to run in fear and be hurt.
- **Walk quietly** through all farms, hamlets and villages, and **leave all gates just as you found them**, wherever they are. Although animals may not be in evidence, the gates *do* have a purpose — generally to keep grazing or herded goats or sheep in — or out of — an area.
- **Protect all wild and cultivated plants.** Don't pick fruit; it is somebody else's livelihood! You'll doubtless be offered some en route, anyhow. Avoid walking over cultivated land.
- **Take all your litter** back with you and dispose of it somewhere suitable.
- When driving, **never block roads or tracks.** Park where you will not inconvenience anyone or cause danger.

1 KATO STALOS • AGIA MARINA • PLATANIAS

See map page 49 and photograph page 26
Distance: 7km/4.5mi; 2h   Grade: easy
Equipment: trainers, sunhat, picnic, water
How to get there: any 🚌 travelling west from Hania on the north coast road (Timetables 5, 6, 7, 8, 9); get off at Kato Stalos (journey 10min)
To return: any 🚌 travelling east from Platanias to Hania on the north coast road (Timetables 5, 6, 7, 8, 9). A bus passes every 15 minutes.

This countryside saunter has been included with those of you in mind who might well be based along western Crete's north coast, not far beyond Hania. Right on your doorstep, here's a pleasant ramble that takes you in a loop via three old villages and enables you to get a good view down over the coast where you are staying.

To **start the walk,** take the turning opposite the Shell petrol station which is signposted 'Stalos 1 km'. Walk up the road, away from the coast, past vineyards and villas; soon the road bends parallel to the sea, before curving towards the hills. When the road forks, take the right-hand fork. Before long, cross a bridge over a bamboo-filled valley and walk on up the other side. Some **15min** into the walk you will notice a lovely old house back on the other side of the valley. Built two and a half centuries ago, it is a classic example of the Turkish style of that era. Looking to the right of the house — beyond its garden, under two or three large trees — you will notice a semicircular hole in the wall. Water for the household flowed from the mountains all those years ago, through this hole and into a stone pool. The water, having been used for washing clothes — and people — was then allowed to drain into the valley to water the fruit trees below the house.

Continue on up towards Stalos. A couple of minutes past the view of the lovely pink house you will pass the cemetery off to the left, shortly after which the village itself comes into sight. Walk past the first *cafeneion* — surrounded by flowers — on the left and take the right turn opposite the next *cafeneion* further on in the village (also on the left). Curve round the building on your right — it has a post box on its wall. Pass a narrow street off to the left and, soon after rounding the next bend, come to a steep concrete track going down left. Before heading down that track, it's worth walking on past the clock tower ahead, to look back at the village of Stalos and get your bearings over the coast and Kato Stalos. The Akrotiri Peninsula rises in the distance to the right, and the island of Agii Theodori can be seen between the houses on the left.

Go back to the track and head off down it. You will

notice a small church on the top of the opposite hillside. When the track runs out, walk left onto a footpath that crosses the hillside through the olive trees. The path joins two tracks at a minor junction at the bottom of the valley. Go straight over the first and continue on the lower track, leaving a small shrine beside the upper track on the right. The track then bends right and passes two large carob trees on the right. It runs the length of the village of Stalos and slowly climbs away. Five minutes later, when the track splits — in line with the clocktower — go up left. It then bends left and you will find yourselves walking parallel to the north coast. When the track reaches a small church, curve left round it, disregarding a fork to the right. The village of Agia Marina comes into sight, dominated by its own large church (**1h**). As you approach the village, look for a shrine; take the minor track beside it that leads down left and across the valley. Cross the bridge and walk up into Agia Marina. When the track joins the asphalted road, turn right. The village opens out into a small square. Turn left in this square, up what becomes a concreted track, leaving a taverna/*cafeneion* to the right. Walk uphill slightly, passing the large village church on the left. Beyond the church, turn down right and then go left almost immediately. As you walk away from Agia Marina you will see the old village of Platanias up on the outcrop of rock ahead. Walk straight on, disregarding a right turn by a shrine and a large, very plain building.

Theodorou Island, home of the Cretan ibex (or *kri-kri* as it is known locally), looms large in the sea on your right. At **1h15min** keep straight ahead, ignoring a left turn. A few minutes later, ignore a cross-tracks. In **1h25min** the track forks in front of a three-storey bulding. Go left here, on a lesser-used track, which peters out almost at once. Clamber up onto the track in front of you and turn right. You will see the pretty blue and white church of Platanias ahead, before rounding a bend in the track. Three minutes later, ignore a turning back to the right. The track leads away from Platanias, but follow it when it curves back towards the village again. Soon it is asphalted. Instead of following the road as it bends left round the church, go straight ahead on the bend, on a concrete track that leads through the village. Explore the village if you like, then return to the route that leads down between the houses and back onto the road. When you meet the road, turn right and descend to the main north coast road and there turn left. The bus stops some 35m/yds ahead, by the kiosk and taxi rank.

2 FROM COAST TO LAKE — STALOS TO AGIA

See photographs pages 19 and 26

Distance: 6km/3.7mi; 1h50min to the lake

Grade: straightforward walk on tracks and roads

Equipment: stout shoes, sunhat, picnic, water

How to get there: as Walk 1, page 46
To return: Walk back to Stalos, or take the Omalos- 🚌(Timetables 3, 6) from the main road at Agia. Departures at 11.00, 15.45, 18.15, 19.00

Short walk: From the main road to the lake and return (2km; 35min). Take the Omalos- 🚌 from Hania to Agia. From the main road, take the right-hand turning to 'Kirtomados 2km'. Soon, stay right where the road forks. Pass a church on the left; the lake is on the right. Stay on the road past a bridge with iron railings, then turn right (1km).

The lake at Agia is a particularly good place to watch birds, a lovely quiet oasis overlooked by the church of Saints Constandinos and Eleni — hence the name Agia, which means 'holy'.

Start out by using the notes for Walk 1, page 46. There's a good *cafeneion*-cum-taverna on the left as you walk into Stalos. Its sign says 'Cretan Feasting'. Walking on, you will pass a turn-off right, in the middle of the village — the route of Walk 1. Beyond this turning, on the far side of the village, keep straight on, ignoring a concrete track leading back into the village on your right and another leading ahead downhill to the right. As you leave Stalos, asphalt gives way to rough track, and you head on through olive groves. Stay on the main track, disregarding any turnings left or right, as you walk on towards the hills. Having climbed slightly, up and away from the coast, the track levels out and then starts sloping gently downhill. The route goes over a concrete bridge and then, about **1h** into the walk, you will pass the small church of Profitis Ilias up to the left of the track. At the junction here, keep on the main route, as it bends down to the right. There is a fine panorama of countryside ahead. Continuing down, you will see a church and graveyard below you. Curl on down past the church and keep on going round to the left.

Some **1h30min** into the walk, you will see your destination down and across to your left. First of all Agia's church comes into view; then you'll see the lake. Round the next bend, the village of Kirtomados comes into range. When you are in line with the first house in Kirtomados, on your right, take a concrete track going down off left through the village. In the midst of the village, at a junction of sorts (where there's a large mulberry tree on the left), weave right and then turn left in front of a large old house with an arched wooden door. Five minutes later, turn left

onto the road. At the next junction, where there is a shrine dedicated to Agios Nektarios, follow the road round to the right, disregarding a track to the left that goes straight on. (That track *does* lead back to Galatas, eventually, but we found it rather dull walking.) Some **1h45min** from the start, take a track going left off the road, just before a bridge with iron railings. Within two to three minutes, when the track runs out, walk up some steps and through cane to the lake.

If you're hoping to do some bird-watching, either sit here or walk along the short path to the right: there are a couple of places where you can edge down through the reeds and be fairly inconspicuous. Then, either retrace your steps to Stalos (**3h40min**), or go back to the road, turn left, walk over the bridge, and keep going until you meet the main Hania road at Agia (**2h10min**), from where you can pick up one of the Omalos or Sougia buses.

3 THERISO • ZOURVA • MESKLA

See map pages 52-53   **Distance:** 8km/5mi; 2h10min

Grade: straightforward, mainly on a track

Equipment: stout shoes, sunhat, picnic, water

How to get there: 🚌 to Theriso (not in the timetables, but departs Hania 07.30 in season; enquire locally); journey time 30 minutes.

To return: 🚌 from Meskla to Hania (not in the timetables, but departs 07.30, 14.00 in season; enquire locally); journey time 30 minutes.

Note: It would have been nice to make this a circular walk, but the people whose animals graze in this area have blocked off the route from Meskla up to Theriso, to prevent walkers using it: *we have been asked to make it clear that the local people prefer you not to walk here.*

Here's a leisurely ramble providing a lovely introduction to the region. The ride from Hania to the start of the walk takes you up via a high-sided gorge lined with plane trees and Spanish chestnuts, to the pretty village of Theriso. Wild flowers cover the hillsides in spring with an almost uncountable variety of blooms. Plan to take a break in Zourva; the taverna is alone worth the walk!

The bus turns round beyond two cafeneions, in front of an old church Theriso. **Start out** by taking the concrete track that goes off to the right of the church (as you face it). The concrete doesn't last for long, as the track climbs away from the village, continuing on beyond it. A streambed is on the left. After about five minutes of gentle climbing, at a

Leaving Zourva, you're soon on a rough track. The flower-lined route affords views over Laki, where the domed church can just be seen in the distance.

hairpin bend signposted right for Zourva, keep left on the main track, which leads downhill. As you approach a bridge (**10min**) over which the main track curves, look straight ahead to find the path leading off; there may be a netting stock control fence across this path. If so, make sure you secure the gate behind you. Follow the path. Soon you may have to negotiate another stock control fence with oleander beside it. The narrow path heads up slightly and continues across the hillside, rising away from the tree-surrounded watercourse.

In **35min** walking, the path divides, just beyond another clump of oleander. Take care to keep to the upper path. Soon the path heads away from the valley. Five minutes further on, you'll see some mesh-fenced terraces up ahead. Follow the path going to the right of the terracing and head up onto the track above (a sign is to the left). At the top go straight ahead on the main track, ignoring forks to the left and right. You will see the village of Laki, with its prominent church, straight ahead of you in the distance. Within moments Zourva will come into sight to the left. Forty minutes later, the track has led you into this village, where there is a simple but 'special' taverna set up on the right — an ideal place for a sustaining brunch of Aimilia's home-made cheese, bread, honey, eggs, salad and mountain tea. Back on the road, you will be through Zourva in three or four minutes. Pass the church on the right, and you've left the village. The road is asphalted for a while; then you're back on track.

Some 25 minutes from Zourva look for a footpath leading right off the track (20-30yds/m before a bend). It makes a steep, but quicker route down the hillside. Waymarking is obvious and, within minutes, you will see the village of Meskla below. Six minutes later, go left onto a track. Soon you will meet the track you were on before the footpath helped you make headway. Walk on downhill to the right; before long, you will pass a sign denoting the village boundary. After a couple of bends, a footpath leads off left and cuts down into the village. Either take that route or continue down on the track. (The track will take you past the massive Panayia Christos Church on the left.)

The sound of running water is all around you by now, and a watercourse accompanies you into Meskla (**2h 10min**). Cross over a bridge and walk a bit further into the village, to find the bus stop. It is outside a *cafeneion,* near an orange metal signboard — just beyond a villa with Corinthian columns, set off the road.

4 DRAKONAS TO THERISO

Distance: 7km/4.5mi; 2h

Grade: straightforward track walking

Equipment: stout shoes, sunhat, picnic, water

How to get there: 🚌 from Hania to Drakonas ('Keramia' bus): departs 14.00. Get off at Drakonas; journey time 1h. (There is also a bus at 06.30, but it's necessary to change en route. It's a long taxi ride, but, if you take that option, make sure you ask for Drakonas-Keramia, because there's another Drakonas, near Kasteli.)

To return: 🚕 from Theriso. It is necessary to ring for a taxi, or pre-arrange one to collect you. See last paragraph of walking notes.

This untaxing country walk starts at the end of a bus route, in the heart of the hills. High mountains frame the left-hand side of the scene, as you walk via vineyards and pine trees to the attractive area around Theriso (where Walk 3 begins).

When the bus stops, finally, in front of the church at Drakonas, **start out** by walking to the left of the church — onto a track. When the track splits, almost immediately, take the right-hand fork. Then, when it divides again, go round to the left, staying on the main track. After a kilometre, reach some houses and follow the track as it curves left. Some **30min** into the walk, keep left at a fork. Continue uphill on the main track, disregarding any tracks off left or right. After some **50min** walking from Drakonas, there is a splendid mountain view over to the right. The mountain peaks will be with you from now on.

As you reach the top of the climb (**1h**), notice two shrines up on the right, where the track divides. Go straight ahead; there are vine terraces down to the left. Shortly after

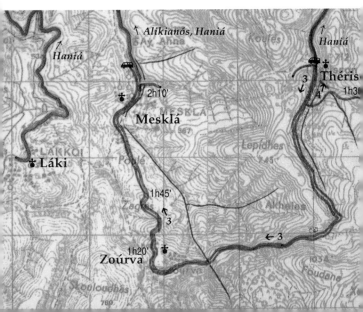

En route from Drakonas to Theriso

this, the track forks again (there is a small sign in Greek indicating Theriso to the left and Drakonas right). Bend hard left and head down towards the vineyards. Close any gates in the netting fences that might be across the track anywhere en route.

At **1h15min** ignore a turning right. Soon pine trees start on your left. Stay right, on the main track, and disregard a smaller track going down left, when there are pine trees either side of your route. About eight minutes after that, keep straight ahead where a track goes back off the main one. From here you can see down into the valley and ahead to Theriso (**1h30min**), beyond the pine trees. As you near the village, the track heads directly away from it (**1h50min**). Then, having rounded a bend back towards the village, once you are beyond a watercourse, look carefully for a netting fence and signs of a footpath going uphill and off left into the undergrowth. This is where Walk 3 starts, and it's worth walking along here for half an hour or so, as it's so pretty, before you head on into Theriso.

Five minutes on towards Theriso from this point, the

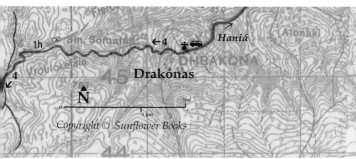

track forks; stay down right. A very old church, set below on the right, heralds the beginning of the village and is where the bus turns round. There are two *cafeneions* here, both on the right, where a taxi could meet you. The one furthest beyond the church is called ΑΡΤΕΜΙΟΥ ΠΑΠΑΔΑΚΗ, in case you want to pre-arrange a taxi.

5 KATOHORI TO STILOS OR NIO HORIO

See map pages 58-59

Distance: 11.3km/7mi; 3h35min to Stilos; 4h to Nio Horio

Grade: moderate to difficult; waymarked gorge walk, clambering necessary in places

Equipment: stout shoes or boots, sunhat, picnic, water

How to get there: Kambi- 🚐 to Katohori (not in the timetables, but departs Hania 06.00 in season; enquire locally); journey 35min.
To return: 🚐 from Stilos to Hania (not in the timetables, departs 16.45 in season; enquire locally); journey takes 30 minutes. *Or* 🚐 from Nio, Horio to Hania (not in the timetables, but departs 11.15, 13.10, 17.30 weekdays, 11.15, 16.20, 18.30 Saturdays/Sundays in season; enquire locally); journey takes 30 minutes.

This a pleasant, but somewhat taxing walk through glorious gorge country. The bus ride from Hania is very well worth the early morning start. The White Mountains rise in an awesome but splendid mass to one side of the route as you climb into the foothills. The gorge itself is an attractive walking route, wedged deeply into the countryside, fringed with leafy plane trees and hemmed with pretty pink oleander bushes near the end of the walk. In parts the walk is demanding, as the gorge floor offers every kind of surface underfoot.

The bus stops just before a bridge where the road curves right (signposted on to Kambi — in Greek). To **start the walk,** cross the road and walk straight on along a road signposted 'Xania (Hania) 21km'. The riverbed that runs through the gorge to Stilos is down to your right. On the first big 'U'-bend left, where there is a miniature concrete church, leave the road and carry straight on along the concrete track. The route forks; go right and walk past a small old church on the right. Four minutes later pass another, large church on the left. Go on into a small square, past a huge telephone pole on the left and a *cafeneion* on the right. Just before the *cafeneion*, take the track leading off *slightly* left; disregard the full left turn. The route makes for a very distinct knob of rock you will notice pointing skyward in the middle distance ahead.

The track, which leads through orange groves, is likely to be wet, particularly in spring. Anywhere around here is a delightful picnic setting; see photograph on page 56. Turn left (**15min**); there may be a cairn marking the start of the route, and soon you will see blue paint waymarks indicating your direction. There are also red dot waymarks along the way. When the track meets the riverbed, cross it. Then, when it comes to the edge of another watercourse, cross over — onto the bank on the other side — and take the footpath ahead, rather than the one going right. You will be led along the edge of the watercourse; make your way along beside it — negotiating a fence, if you encounter one. In less than **1h** the landscape opens out somewhat; then the towering sides of the gorge close in on us again.

At **2h30min** there is a serious piece of negotiation necessary; take your time. After **2h50min** you will notice the gorge coming to an end, as the countryside opens out. The walk continues in and beside the riverbed. And at **3h05min** into the walk, the waymarking leads us up to the right, away from the oleander-lined riverbed and onto an

On a hot day the leafy depths of this pretty inland gorge near Katohori provide welcome shade (Picnic 5b).

earth track. Within three to four minutes keep straight on (where a track goes off right). A minute further on the track divides: go down left, crossing back over the riverbed. Blue arrows direct you up right, ahead. Climb the small hill and, at the top, bend round between the houses — greeting the interested owners — and turn right onto a concrete track (**3h15min**). Disregard a path going right towards fields a minute later.

After **3h20min** you will meet the road, bordered by olive groves. You can wait for the bus here, but you'll find a *cafeneion* in the village. Turn right and very shortly pass the sign for Stilos. Cross the bridge, pass a shrine to St Pantelimon on a curve in the road, and continue into the centre of the village. Rather than sit about in Stilos until the late afternoon bus, why not walk to Nio Horio just 25 minutes away? Here you can pick up one of the more regular buses to Hania — or a taxi. The bus stops opposite the kiosk which you will see as you approach the village. If you decide to wait in Stilos, there are two bus stops, both marked with signs. One is opposite the large shady open area, outside a *cafeneion*; the other is a little further on, opposite the Neo Demokratia headquarters, marked with a blue and white sign.

Enjoy Picnic 5a here, near Katohori. From this picnic setting, surrounded by orange groves, there are views towards Kambi and the White Mountains (Levka Ori). Kambi is the starting point for Walk 6.

Distance: 18.5km/11.5mi; 5h35min

Grade: very strenuous; for the adventurous and fit

Equipment: walking boots, long trousers, long socks, anorak, sunhat, compass, picnic, water

How to get there: 🚌 to Kambi (not in the timetables, but departs Hania 06.00 in season; enquire locally); journey takes 40 minutes. *To return:* 🚌 from Kambi to Hania (not in the timetables, but departs Kambi 14.45; enquire locally).

I f you have come to Crete prepared to spend some nights away from your base, consider staying in Kambi the night before starting this hike. It's a very pleasant, quiet village with a relaxed atmosphere. There is a bus up to Kambi at crack of dawn, but as this trek is a real energy-tester, you might find it helpful to be on the spot in the early morning ... particularly if you fancy turning it into an expedition.* As the success of this walk relies on compass readings, do choose a clear day, when the mountains are easily visible and the views are sure to be good.

The bus stops in the village square, by the church. **Set off:** walk right, past the church, on a rough track. (The bus continues in the same direction en route for Madaro.) There is a *cafeneion* straight ahead of you called 'ΗΠΡΟΟΔΟΣ'. Walk to the right of it; it is a meeting place for the village elders and a nice place to rest and wait for the return bus to Hania. Take a compass reading on the corner by the *cafeneion,* as you pass it. Face the mountains you are heading towards, which are due south, and notice, in particular, the tree-covered slopes of a ravine in the distance (see captions to the photographs on pages 60 and 61). Then continue on the track, disregarding a lesser track left passed a few minutes later. Beyond a blue shrine on the right, come to some very pretty, lush countryside; this is a fine picnic spot. Masses of wildflowers line the route, and it is surrounded by fig trees, walnut trees, vines and olives. Pass another *cafeneion* that has rows of potted plants and flowers along its length, and a shrine — both on the right-hand side of the track. Directly afterwards, take the right-hand fork.

Soon after forking right, look up to the spread of mountains again and take note once more of the dark 'V' of the tree-lined ravine, almost in the centre of the view ahead —

---

*It is possible to hire a guide in Kambi who will show you the area *beyond* the EOS hut at Volika, which is our point of return. You would stay overnight at the hut (taking your own provisions), which is otherwise locked. Arrange it via the EOS office beneath Olympic Airways in Hania or at the *cafeneion* in Kambi run by Georgios Nikolioudakis.

perhaps referring again to the photograph captions on pages 60 and 61. Turn left at the T-junction (**10min**), pass a field of vines on your right, and then turn right. Close any stock control gates that you encounter en route. When the track runs out (**25min**) and two footpaths lead off, go left. There are about three waymark arrows along the first stages of the path, but they soon run out, and you must make your way up the hillside, taking any one of several possible paths. Keep near the fence on the left until, as you draw level with a line of low bumpy hills on your left in the distance, the path heads away from the fence slightly. Continue onwards and upwards, remembering the direction in which you are heading. Keep to the right-hand side along a fence going up the hillside, carefully closing any stock control

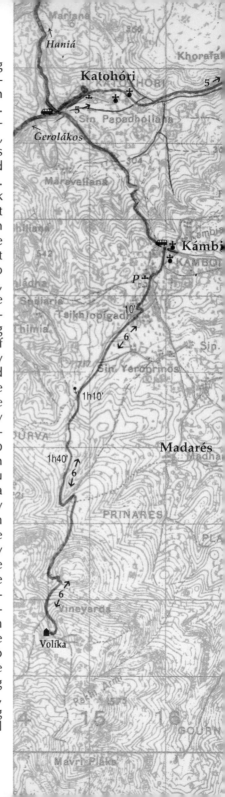

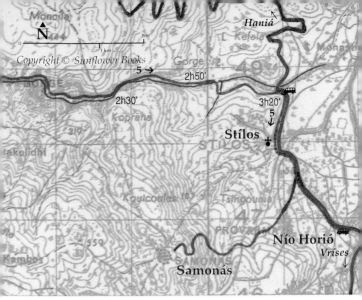

fence behind you, if you have to go through one. Look ahead and get your bearings: there is one prominent, domed mountain in the distance. Between you and it is a hill which is high on the left and low on the right. Directly to your right, the hillside shows signs of track running along it, just below the top. The fence is still 15-20m/yds away on your left. Head towards the high, left-hand end of the hill ahead; the route climbs steeply.

After **45min** walking, turn round and get your bearings for the return. *This is important.* Beyond Souda Bay, in the distance, the Akrotiri (airport) mast is visible. At the left end of the same peninsula, where the mountainside seems to fall into the sea, is Stavros (shown in the photograph on page 25). Further left, pick out the island of Theodorou, just off the north coast at Platanias and, beyond that, the Rodopou Peninsula. Then *take note of Kambi's position very carefully.* These precautions are to save you wading through thistles and thorny burnet on your way back down to the village.

Further on into the climb up this first hillside (**50min**), when there are more folds of mountains visible ahead, pause to take stock yet again and identify your destination and route. The large domed mountain ahead has trees down the left side of its top. Two 'bumps' from that one, to the left, find a mountain with trees all over its summit (at the right of the photograph on page 60). Head towards this latter. There are huge bare mountains beyond and left of it.

As you come to the top of a rise, identify the route to

The lone wild pear tree at the right of this photograph is a useful landmark. You are aiming for the 'V' in the mountains to the left of the photograph, shown in close-up opposite.

your destination, which is via the 'V'-shaped ravine, with trees down both its sloping sides. (Before you reach the ravine, and the final climb to the Volika refuge, there is a small gulley to be negotiated.) There *is* waymarking, but it is more directional than an indication of an actual *path* and, as several people have had a 'go' at waymarking, it's best to just keep your goal in sight and think where you are heading. So, set off in the direction of the ravine: from the rise a path leads beside a short, low stone wall, heading for the mountains. This path leads to the right of a lone tree — a wild pear — that forks at the top; it's a good landmark, especially on the return journey. This tree is shown at the right of the photograph above. Stand under the tree for a moment and look up into the ravine. Sharp eyes will be able to pick out the refuge hut, beyond the tree line; it's just in the centre of the photograph opposite. Now is the time to decide if you want to go all the way, because it's going to get steep!

Just beyond the wild pear tree, the path goes through a break in the fence and then forks. Take the right fork and very soon (**1h10min**) the path leads to the left of a well and a drinking trough. You will see the letters ΕΟΣ and a red arrow painted on a boulder to the right of the path. Follow the sporadic, directional waymarking; **1h30min** from Kambi you will be at the edge of a small wooded gulley. You can see the path going up the far side of it, leading on to the ravine and the climb to Volika. Seven to eight minutes later, having crossed the gulley and taken a breather, cross the flat area beyond. (There are waymarks just above eye level on rocks about 15m/yds apart, either side of the route.) Twenty minutes from the wooded gulley, having negotiated some sharp, pale grey rock, you look up the ravine and towards the final ascent. Good waymarking now leads you up the very steep right-hand side of the ravine. Trees en route provide shade and resting places. After climbing for twenty minutes or so, the path leads you to the other (left) side of the ravine. Ten minutes later it re-crosses, bringing you back to the right. Thirty-five minutes from starting up the ravine, come to a pleasant green, wooded flat area; the ravine appears to have come to an end. But follow the waymarking on and up. The ravine becomes a gulley, wedged between layered rock to the left of the route.

Just under an hour from the start of the final ascent the Volika hut comes into sight. Five minutes later the path crosses the gulley on the layered rock. The waymarking is very occasional over this last stretch but, looking at your destination, approach it from the left to find easiest access. By **3h30min** from Kambi you will have the satisfaction of reaching the hut.

The return journey should take much less time, although a large proportion of it requires careful walking and close attention to direction. It will take about an hour to get to the bottom of the ravine. Make your way back and, when you reach the top of the small, wooded gulley on the far side of the ravine, head due north — *not* northeast. Be sure to go far enough in a northerly direction before turning towards Kambi; wait until you can actually see the village and route on which you started the climb, before heading down towards it. Walk back into Kambi and have a well-deserved rest in the *cafeneion,* where you can wait for the bus to Hania.

Here's a closer view of our goal, the Volika refuge. It's in the centre of the photograph, just above the tree line.

7 GEORGIOUPOLI CIRCUIT

Distance: 14km/8.7mi; 4h15min   See also photograph page 27
Grade: straightforward, but with some overgrown path to negotiate
Equipment: stout shoes, sunhat, picnic, water, swimming things, long trousers/socks
How to get there and return: any Rethimnon or Iraklion 🚌 (Timetables 1, 2) to Georgioupoli and back; journey time 45 minutes

Georgioupoli is a pleasant place, not only for walking, but for eating and swimming as well. Doing the whole of this walk needs a somewhat intrepid nature, as parts of the path are overgrown and scratchy — downright tiresome in places! Going only as far as the splendid view at Likotinara might be enough for most people, but it is satisfying to complete the walk.

Get off the bus, which stops opposite the turning to Georgioupoli (Walk 8 ends here), cross over the road, and go on into the village square, where **the walk starts**. Go straight across the square, disregarding turnings off to the left and right. The road leads down over a bridge which spans the fishing harbour shown on page 27. There's a lovely view out to sea on your right and up to the mountains on your left. Walk away from the village, passing taverna signs right and left. Some **10min** from the square, disregard a track going off right and, a few minutes later, ignore another rough track going off right (there is a mulberry and a pine tree set back from the road on it). Then take a track that turns right, going off just after a bend in the road. About 15 paces from the road you pass some tall conifers. The old grassy track starts to climb and, in a couple of minutes, it meets the road again. Carry on up the hill. Disregard a path going off left on the next bend and, on the next big bend left, a narrow footpath leads steeply up to the right. Follow it up. Halfway up the rise, meet another footpath crossing the one you're on and go right on this well-established, wide stony path. When it forks, go left and, in a couple of minutes, you emerge in front of the Panorama Taverna at Argirimouri; it's to the right of the road (**45min**). Walk to the right, passing the front of the taverna, and you'll see a track going off to the left. Look for waymarking which starts along here.

Some **50min** into the walk, after a concreted section, as the track you are on

Colourful hillsides near Georgioupoli

62

bends to the right, look for a footpath off to the left. It's very important, by the way, that you keep looking for the waymarking, as it's easy to go astray across the hillside ahead. If at any time you appear to lose it, retrace your steps or make sure you find it before going on. The path starts in a northerly direction, but very soon heads right (east) — look for fencing up the hillside; the path runs beside it. Once you've found the discernible path, you'll find it heads uphill with a wall on its right-hand side. Stay with the waymarking and the wall. The path appears to divide when it comes to the corner of the wall; stay right, by the wall, heading in a north-northeasterly direction, before swinging round to head north — away from the wall for a while. Paths appear to go off occasionally; follow the waymarking. At a T-junction in the path, turn left. *Then make sure that you go no further right on the hillside than the line of the tavernas below you.*

Some **1h15min** into the walk, look for helpful cairns, as well as waymarking. As the way levels out, you will find yourself on the crest of the hill; stone walls with netting running along the top of them lie to your right. You may have to go through a netting gate at the top; remember to close it, if that's how you find it. Soon you will be able to see over to the sea. The path heads slightly downhill. The dwellings over to your right are part of Likotinara, where you are heading — for a fantastic view. At **1h35min** into the walk, the footpath hits track and, five minutes later, look for a small path heading off right, towards the houses. Take it and, when you meet a concrete road, turn right and walk for four to five minutes, to the viewing terrace. You can just see Georgioupoli over to the right (**1h45min**).

Turn round and walk back, passing the place where the footpath came onto the road. You could choose to retrace your steps from here. Walking on, you will soon come to a

forked junction on asphalt road. Right goes to Kefalas ('2km/Κεφαλαζ'). Go left, towards Litsardes ('4km'). Pass a sign indicating you are leaving Likotinara and, about eight minutes later (**2h05min**), walk past the sign at the start of Selia and go on into the village. Three minutes into it, at the junction, follow the road as it bends round to the right. In a couple of hundred metres (yards), opposite a basketball area, look for a track going off left, by a shrine at the corner of a house. Very soon the track becomes a way-marked cobbled path, heading south. Within five minutes you will notice that the path runs above and parallel to the road. This is where you could do with long trousers, as the way is very overgrown and prickly in places.

Some **2h25min** into the walk, you will be able to see the sea again at Georgioupoli, edging round a corner on the left. Follow the waymarking, taking care of any fencing. The path winds down onto the road, near a big bend to the right. Head left, away from the road, and walk along the top of a terraced plot. At the end of the terrace, it may be necessary to step up over a netting fence, to continue on the path. Keep an eye on the waymarking and continue across the hill-side, in the direction of Georgioupoli. Watch out for cairns as well as waymarking: when you see two placed together (**2h**

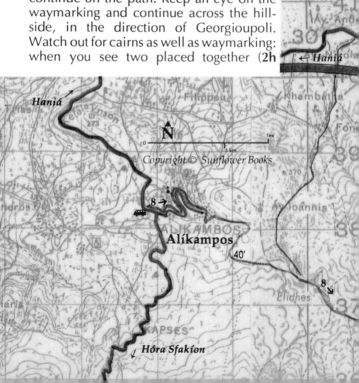

Copyright © Sunflower Books

50min), rather than go between them, leave them both on your right. Look out for what seems like a solitary carob tree: there is a waymark beneath it, and another the far side of it. But in fact this is the beginning of a grove of carob trees, and the waymarking leads under and around a fair number of them — go under the first, to the left of the second, skirt round the next to the right, go to the left of the next, and then under some others, goat height. Just keep the waymarking in sight! By **3h10min** the path starts heading downhill to a flattish area — look for the waymarking that leads up on the other side.

Over the rise you are likely to be confronted suddenly by barking dogs (one of them an Alsatian), as this is where Giorgios — a cosmopolitan shepherd — keeps his sheep, chickens, peacocks, and dogs. The dogs make a noise if they are there — that's

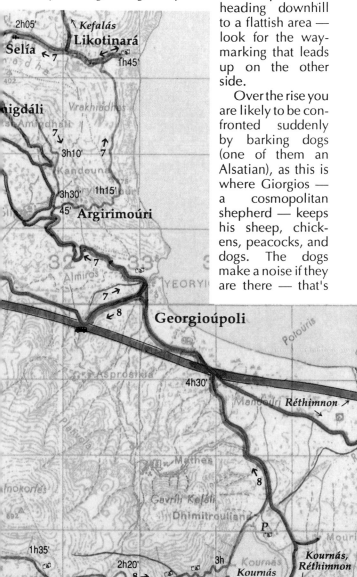

their job; but they are unlikely to go for you; they are used to passers-by. Giorgios came out and quieted them when we walked by, and then we were treated to bread, yogurt, juicy oranges and copious quantities of raki .... Your route goes straight across the front of his buildings and then heads down off right. Beyond the area in front of the 'farm' buildings, a concrete track bends round to the right, and you can see the road. There's a waymarked short-cut footpath down to the road; it goes off left under an olive and a carob tree. Turn left on the main (asphalt) road (**3h 30min**).

Five minutes later you will be back at the junction outside the Panorama Taverna at Argirimouri, just beyond where the track leads down to Georgioupoli, the way you came. Take the familiar rough track which leaves the road off to the left and, when you are back on the road again, turn left. You will be back at the bridge **4h05min** after setting out. Walk back through the village, arriving at the road and bus stop ten minutes later (**4h15min**).

Walk 8: Some 40 minutes into the walk, Alikampos is well below you, as you head for the hills along this flower-lined track.

8 ALIKAMPOS • KOURNAS LAKE • GEORGIOUPOLI

See map pages 64-65; see photographs page 27 and opposite

Special note: Women are advised not to wear shorts along the path of this walk, and you need to take care near the lake if the shepherds' dogs are guarding the animal pens. (We had been planning to cut this walk from this new edition. But so many users have written to us and spoken to us, urging us to keep the walk in the book, that we have done so. When we first traced the route, we had a problem with shepherds at the highest point in the walk, and people using the book have had problems with dogs near the lake. Since publication of the first edition, however, the route has been waymarked; we have established that the local people are happy for people to walk there; the errant gentleman has moved on; and they've stopped hunting so, although there are still dogs near the lake occasionally, they are the sheep-herding types.)

Distance: 13km/8mi; 4h30min

Grade: moderate to strenuous — a combination of an easy track and a steep footpath requiring agility

Equipment: stout shoes, sunhat, picnic, water, swimming things

How to get there: 🚌 to the Alikampos turn-off, 7km south of Vrises (Hora Sfakion bus, Timetable 4): departs Hania 08.30, 11.00, 14.00; journey takes 50 minutes.
To return: 🚌 from Georgioupoli to Hania (Timetables 1, 2): departs every 30 minutes; journey takes 50 minutes.

As soon as you feel ready for a testing walk, embark on this one. It combines straightforward walking in pleasant countryside with a good measure of downhill scrambling in a dry ravine. The lake at Kournas is the only freshwater lake on Crete, and it makes an attractive goal.

Ask the bus conductor to drop you at the turning for Alikampos. **Start the walk** by the signposted left turn. It leads away from the splendid panorama of the White Mountains, which by now will be a familiar backdrop. The second major bend is hairpin-tight, and there is a water reservoir off to the left. Continue on the road, keeping left when it forks, and it will lead you into a small square at Alikampos. There is a war memorial on the right and a *cafeneion* beyond it, straight ahead. Turn right in front of the *cafeneion* and start walking away from the village. After a few minutes, pass a shrine on the right and keep going — ignoring a smaller road going off to the right. You will pass another shrine on the left (just past another road leading off left). Keep going, now on rough track, passing another turning off left. By **40min** Alikampos is well below you, as you head for the hills along the flower-lined track shown opposite.

At **1h35min** into the walk, having passed via Dafno-korfes (the hill on the left; 692m) and Halara (1968m; slightly further off to the right), you come to a crossing track (just before the top of the pass). Bear right. Five minutes later the track peters out, just beyond a shepherds' dwelling. Look for the footpath to the left of two olive-tree trunks. It strikes out in an east-southeasterly direction. Within four or five minutes the north coast will be spread out in the distance below, off to the left. The path heads downhill beneath a pear tree; keep left where it splits and walk coastwards. Tread carefully; the path is very steep and you may well find it necessary to scramble. At the bottom, head to the right of the obvious hillock in front of you; then go slightly left and downwards, soon turning directly to face the sea.

By **2h20min,** the path passes an animal shelter on the left. Look right and head towards the paddock below. Cross the paddock and continue on out the far side, following the footpath, which soon heads downwards again — it's rough, but well waymarked. It leads under and round a huge olive tree. Beyond the tree there is an open flat area. Walk along its right-hand edge. Once across the flat, the path descends dramatically and needs *careful negotiation*. This is where the real scrambling starts.

Suddenly the lovely green and turquoise lake at Kournas comes into sight, and there are some good places to perch to take in the tremendous view. The route leads across the left side of the ravine. Go under a spreading fig; then make for a huge curving carob. From here, continue down to the dry streambed. *Watch your step.* At **3h05min** a more discernible footpath leads away from the ravine, but it is only one of several paths through the shrubs. As long as you head towards the lake you can't go wrong, but an obvious route leads via a couple of shepherds' buildings and a sheep fold, and from there to the lake. It divides just beyond the sheep fold; go right. On reaching the lake (some 1h20min from passing the shepherds' dwelling at the beginning of the footpath), go left on the track that hems its perimeter. It's lovely to swim in this clear water.

At the end of the lake (**3h40min**), the track bends round beside a building on your right. If there is a fence here, get onto the right-hand side of it. Follow the track to the road, ten minutes away. Here turn left along the road, until you see a sign (**4h30min**) indicating Rethimnon right and Hania left. Turn left. You are on the old road, heading for Georgioupoli, over a bridge crossing the main highway. Either have a swim at Georgioupoli before the bus ride back to Hania, or walk onto the main highway, where you will see the bus stop (frequent buses into Hania).

9 THE PRASSANOS GORGE

Distance: 13km/8mi; 4h05min

Grade: One section requires agility and a bit of careful scrambling; if the winter has been wet, the narrowest part of the gorge may be impassable in spring. See warning in the **STOP PRESS**.

Equipment: stout shoes, sunhat, water, swimming things

How to get there: any 🚌 going to Rethimnon or Iraklion (Timetables 1, 2); get off at the Rethimnon bus station. Journey takes 1h from Hania to Rethimnon. Then take a bus to Amari (different bus station); departures 06.45, 14.30 (journey time 30min) or a taxi (20min).

To return: 🚌 There are frequent town buses where the walk ends on the old road outside Rethimnon.

This gorge is an awe-inspiring and inviting sight as it carves a swathe through the countryside to the coast by Rethimnon. It has obviously been created by great force — as you'll see from the massive boulders en route. The landscape around is very open and pleasing to look at, making a good, accessible walk.

Ask for 'Prassanos', which is the gorge, or Mirthios, and the bus will drop you at a junction where Mirthios is indicated off to the right. From where the bus stops, **start the walk** by going on for about 50 metres (yards). Then look for a concrete track curving around left off the road. (A taxi will drop you by the track, if you say you're going to 'walk Prassano'. As you turn onto the track, you will be facing the huge gorge itself; the landscape is tremendous here, open and grand.

The concrete runs out in 50 metres or so. When the now-rough track splits, take the right-hand, more used fork, and follow it as it bends down through acres of ferns.

Particularly well sited if you're staying in Rethimnon, Prassanos — another of Crete's spectacular gorges — offers a dramatic-looking invitation. This photograph was taken from the top of a ridge not far beyond Prasies (Car tour 8).

Some **10min** from the start you will see a farm building. Approach it and leave it on your right. Then pass another breeze-block building to your right and continue on downhill on the insignificant-looking track. It runs under telephone wires and loops down towards a watercourse. Cross the watercourse and head on and over the next, narrower streambed which is lined with plane trees. Within a few paces, look for a small footpath going off right, along the left-hand bank of the streambed. It's not very distinct, but follow it as best you can and, in about eight to ten minutes, you will cross over the stream and go up onto the right bank. This is a favourite haunt of lizards, so don't be surprised by any darting and slithering about.

You will see another line of plane trees, running from right to left, ahead. Walk (on no particular path) towards the middle of the line, which is to the right of where you are. Then, as you near the treeline, look for a distinct way down to the broad riverbed below: it is a steep path, leading through ferns and plane trees. Turn left and walk along the riverbed. In somewhat under **1h**, turn left again and continue along the riverbed. Five minutes later you

This delightful old bridge over the Platys River in the Amari Valley (Car tour 8) is the lovely setting for Picnic CT8. Psiloritis rises in the background. Walk 28 explores part of this area, which sheltered many Resistance fighters during World War II.

will see the head of the gorge to your left. Turn towards it and, another five minutes further on, you will be walking in a northerly direction along the right-hand side of the riverbed. Some **1h05min** into the walk, a wall of the gorge rears up dramatically on your left. You may see an occasional crab and get faint whiffs of sea air around here.

Some 15 minutes from where you passed the first gorge wall, the riverbed swings northwest. Fantastic rock faces now rear up all round you. At **1h25min** from the start of the walk the gorge makes another bend left (northwest) and you are faced with big, water-smoothed boulders. Before very long the gorge looks as though it is virtually impassable, as you see a 12 foot (4 metre) drop in front of you. You *can* slither down, slightly to the right. But for those of you who like to feel firm ground underfoot, go back until you find a way up what has been the right-hand side of the riverbed. Head uphill 30 feet (12 metres) or so, and scramble along the side of the gorge, which seems like a rock-slide. Move beyond a plane tree, an oleander bush, and another plane tree (beyond two large boulders that seem to be in your way). After that, you can scramble back down onto the floor of the gorge (**1h50min**). Phew!

Continue on, knowing that (unless there has been recent storm damage) there aren't any more sections like that, and enjoy the splendour of the gorge. The gorge narrows again (**2h45min**) and, 15 minutes later, you are beyond the main part of it, still on the riverbed, but in open countryside. After **3h30min** look for a path striking up left from the riverbed. It goes up onto the left bank, where an olive grove begins. Follow the path through the olives; you may see several paths, but they all lead the same way. Five minutes' walking will bring you up beyond a stone wall, onto another level. Ahead you may well see some wrecked cars, rusting in heaps, unless by happy chance they've been moved. Go on through the mess of metal.

The path turns into track as you move through the grove, and the riverbed, which is nearby on the right, becomes somewhat unattractive, but you can soon see the sea beyond (**3h40min**). A lovely old gently-arching bridge spans the riverbed. The track leads onto a concrete road. Turn right — the road soon becomes asphalted. Walk on, passing some apartments on the left and a cement works on the right. Well, there are views, and there are views! Continue under a bridge that carries the main north coast road, and turn left onto the old road. The bus stop is beyond the sign for Missiria; alternatively, hail a taxi.

10 RETHIMNON • AGIA IRINI • KAPADIANA • CHROMONASTIRI • MYLI • (RETHIMNON)

Grade: moderate   **See map pages 70-71 and photograph page 20**

Distance: 15km/9.3mi; 4h (to Myli, where you could order a taxi to Rethimnon) or 23km/14.3mi; 6h15min (to Rethimnon)

Equipment: stout shoes, sunhat, long socks, picnic, water

How to get there and return: any Hania/Rethimnon- 🚐 to Rethimnon station and back (Timetables 1, 2); journey time 1 hour

This walk takes us from the busy harbour town of Rethimnon up into the countryside behind, where we find two old villages well off the beaten track. Then on to Myli, where water has taken over from people, leaving the village dramatically deserted — bar one or two stalwarts.

Start out by leaving the ticket office of the Iraklion/ Hania bus station in Rethimnon on your left and walking slightly uphill. Take the first turning left, down to the main road (Pavlou Kountourioti). Turn right and continue for a kilometre. The road will rise slightly as it leaves the centre of town. As it opens out, look for a turning right (Theotokopoulou) which has a kiosk set up off the road you are on, at its corner. You won't see the sign until you are past the kiosk. Walk straight on up the hill, disregarding turnings left and right. You'll soon see the small church of Profitis Ilias perched on a hill. Some 15 minutes from where you turned off the main road, there is a house on a large bend in the road. Walk just to the right of the house on a bit of rough track — it cuts a bend out of your ascent. Arriving at the road again, by a shrine, take the track that goes right to the church. This is a lovely picnic setting, from where you'll have a splendid view over Rethimnon.

When you're ready to move on, go back down to the road, turn left and, within 80 metres (yds), take a concrete and stone track that veers off and up to the right of the road.

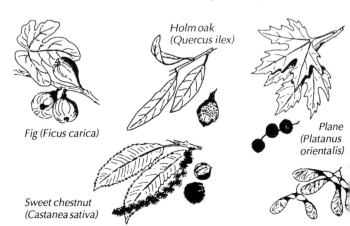

Holm oak
(Quercus ilex)

Fig (Ficus carica)

Plane
(Platanus orientalis)

Sweet chestnut
(Castanea sativa)

Before long the concrete ends, and rough track is underfoot. There is a fresh-smelling pine wood on your left. Disregard the track going off left and other trails through the pines; keep straight on. Soon the way levels out. Every pace immerses you further in the countryside. Some ten minutes from the road, disregard a turning off left and keep walking via olive trees and vineyards. A minute later, keep straight on — where a well-concreted track leads up right, and a rough track goes left just ahead of you. Shortly after this cross-tracks of sorts, it looks as if the track you are on runs out, but it goes steeply downhill and narrows to footpath for a few metres where it crosses a watercourse and goes up the other side, soon passing some fig trees.

An hour from the main road in Rethimnon, meet a T-junction — the track ahead is concreted. Turn right. A good deal of building is going on around here, on the outskirts of Agia Irini. Walk into and through the village, **1h20min** from Rethimnon. On the far side of the village, meet a tarmac road; turn left and walk downhill. You will become aware of a church perched far up on the top of Vrissinas, the mountain in the distance. It is a Minoan peak sanctuary — and our goal on Walk 11. Some **1h40min** from Rethimnon, take the concreted road which forks right and is signposted in Greek 'Καπαδιανα 2km'. The turning is just before the village of Roussospiti. In five minutes the concreted road forks after a major bend; stay left and then go left again on what has become tarmac road. Disregard tracks off to various building works.

As you near Kapadiana, look for a turning off right (**2h05min**); there are waymark signs on the road and on a rock (you'll see them when you look back from just beyond them). Just off the road here is a leafy, cool, open

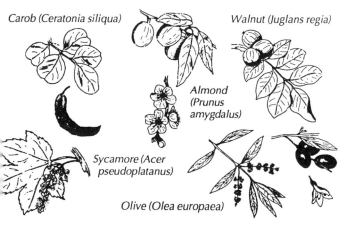

Carob (Ceratonia siliqua)

Walnut (Juglans regia)

Almond (Prunus amygdalus)

Sycamore (Acer pseudoplatanus)

Olive (Olea europaea)

area, where there is a spring. Walk 11, the ascent to Vrissinas, starts here. For the walk we are on now, have a rest in the shade if you like, then continue on into Kapadiana. The road forks: go right, and the concrete road runs out and becomes a waymarked path; soon there are stone walls either side. There is a small church on your right (**2h20min**) and, just beyond it, the path leads onto track. Turn right and, five or six paces on, turn off left onto a lovely path leading through the olive groves. All along the right-hand side is a wooded ravine. The path opens out (**2h30min**) and you can see Chromonastiri straight ahead. Shortly afterward the path leads down onto track. Turn right and, within paces, look for the path going left down and back off the track; it's loose and stony underfoot. The path meets track again (**2h45min**); go down right and cross over two small concrete bridges. The track becomes (mostly cobbled) path again beyond an orange grove on your left and starts climbing uphill towards the village.

When you meet a road (**2h55min**), cross over and walk past houses on a concreted track. In two to three minutes, rather than going straight on, take a left turn, which leads to the village square and a couple of *cafeneions*. Head across the square, past a church on the left and an obelisk on the right, and turn left on the road (**3h05min**) beyond it, to go downhill. Very soon, just after a shrine on the right, take the track that goes off right. In spring masses of daisies line the route. When you meet the road again, turn left and walk downhill, following a large bend to the right, round the end of a deep verdant ravine filled with chestnut and fig trees. Ten minutes after joining the road you will see a stone church/shrine and steps leading off right (**3h40min**), down into the ravine. Take them and, at the bottom, as you come to the old church, go down right towards the water channel. There's a fresh water spring just beyond the church, should you want to fill your bottle. (Myli, the name of this ravine and the deserted village in it, comes from the many water mills in the area.) Follow the path that goes beside, in and over the water channel. When the path forks, go left over a concrete bridge and on up the left-hand side of the ravine. To explore the ruined village of Myli, walk on for five minutes. Then return to this fork. Once over the bridge, you will see a path heading up right from the ravine. Up on the road, turn right and head for the coast and Rethimnon (8km); it's worth hitching a lift for this bit. Alternatively, walk up into the newer part of Myli, above the road to the left, and order a taxi.

11 VRISSINAS, MINOAN PEAK SANCTUARY

See map page 70-71, photograph page 30, and Stop Press page 136

Distance: 6km/3.7mi; 2h   **Grade:** fairly strenuous

Equipment: stout shoes, sunhat, picnic, water, long trousers or socks

How to get there and return: 🚌 to Rethimnon (see Walk 10); then taxi to Kapadiana. (A bus goes to Roussospiti, 2km from Kapadiana, at 14.30, but it does not return to Rethimnon until 06.30 the next day.)

This is one of those hikes that gives a great sense of achievement and a fantastic view. And it's particularly satisfying to see the mountain from all around and know that you've been up there! The local people make pilgrimages to Vrissinas at Easter and other festivals.

Leave the road before the village of Kapadiana or, if you've come by bus, walk back out of the village towards Roussospiti for a couple of hundred metres (yards) and look for the waymark arrow pointing into the trees. There is waymarking on the road and a rock indicating a spring off left, as you come from the village, and **the walk starts** here. Beyond the spring the waymarking leads off up to the left; keep left within a few metres (where rough cobbles stop, and a path appears to head off right). Within two to three minutes the path comes up onto track; turn right and walk up the track. On the first big bend, head right,where waymarking directs you to onto a shaded well-cobbled path. The cobbles end before long. Keep the waymarking in sight. At this stage your goal, the mountain church, is out of sight.

Some **30min** from the start the path meets track again. Walk left and round a bend in the track; then, within a minute, look for the waymarked path off right again. Head up the steep north side of the mountain via shady oaks. In spring this part of the walk is thickly edged with glorious, bright yellow Jerusalem sage (see page 30), and there is pretty mauve *Cistus* everywhere.

Some **40min** from the start the path divides, but you must look very carefully here. You need to go left, but three inviting blue crosses may entice you off to the right. The crosses mean *don't* go right — they aren't waymarks, exactly! Go left and continue across and up the hillside on well-defined path. For a while you are walking parallel with Kapadiana and Chromonastiri. Within about **1h 15min** you will have zig-zagged to the summit sanctuary, from where there are wonderful views over the north coast and Rethimnon.

Return to Kapadiana the same way and either find your transport there, or walk on to Myli (see Walk 10).

12 GOUVERNETO AND KATHOLIKOU

See map page 82; see photograph page 24

Distance: 5km/3mi; 1h30min

Grade: moderate to strenuous, with a steep descent to Katholikou Monastery and a correspondingly steep ascent back to Gouverneto

Equipment: stout shoes, sunhat, picnic, water, swimming things, torch, suitable dress for entrance to the monastery (shorts are not permitted). **NB:** Gouverneto Monastery is closed from 14.00-17.00.

How to get there and return: This walk is best approached by car (see Car tour 4, page 26). Otherwise it's a fairly long taxi journey. Bus times are very inconvenient: 🚌 to Agia Triada (not in the timetables, but departs Hania 06.30 or 13.00 daily in season); journey takes 30 minutes. Buses run Agia Triada to Hania 07.00 and 13.30 in season.

The Akrotiri Peninsula, mushrooming out into the sea east of Hania, invites exploration. This walk follows an ancient path, originally traced by a hermit who, in the eleventh century, founded what is considered to be the island's earliest monastery, Moni Katholikou. It's a steep downhill route, but you can go on to the sea for a refreshing dip before climbing back up.

Leaving your car on the seaward side of Moni Gouverneto, **start out** by taking the path (by a hillock) leading down the hillside towards the sea. A red arrow on a shrine to your left will direct you initially. In **5min** you enjoy the lovely views shown on page 24. Continue down (sometimes on rough steps) and — by some ruins — leave the path and turn right to a cave (**10min**), with a chapel dedicated to Panagia Arkoudiotissa at its entrance and a huge, bear-shaped stalagmite in its centre.

Continuing the walk, go over a low rubble wall and head on down left, towards a gap in the cliffs ahead. This path rejoins the one you left earlier, to see the cave. Turn right and continue down the hill. After **20min** the upper part of Moni Katholikou comes into sight. Reach another cave, halfway down a set of well-hewn steps. Near the bottom of the hill, a larger cave appears: this one contains, in its furthest recess, the grave of the hermit saint.

Now descend to the bridge below. Cross to the far left- or right-hand corner of the top of the bridge and scramble down the rocks to the dry streambed below; it leads to the sea. (Access is easier from the left corner, although on the way back it's easier getting up onto the bridge from the right.) By **45min** you will see the sea ahead. Getting to the water isn't very straightforward just at the end of your descent, but walk round to the left. Here it's perfectly feasible to get to the sea, from an old slipway.

To return, retrace your steps back uphill.

13 THE RODOPOU PENINSULA: RODOPOS • AGIOS IOANNIS GIONIS • RODOPOS

Distance: 18km/11.3mi; 5h30min

Grade: fairly straightforward, with one long, steep descent and a gradual end-of-walk climb. Almost no shade en route

Equipment: stout shoes, sunhat, cover-up protection from the sun, picnic, water

How to get there: 🚌 to Rodopos (not in the timetables, but departs Hania 07.30, 13.30 in season; enquire locally). Alternative: 🚌 to Kolimbari (Timetables 7, 8; departs Hania frequently) and taxi from there to Rodopos (the taxi rank is opposite the Hotel Rosmarie).

To return: Taxi from Rodopos to Kolimbari (telephone from the *cafeneion* in the village square), then 🚌 to Hania (Timetables 7, 8); these buses running between Kasteli and Hania are frequent.

One can't fail to notice the Rodopou Peninsula on the map of Crete, jutting out into the sea with the Gramvousa Peninsula — rather like a rabbit's ears. The peninsulas invite exploration. This is one of our favourite routes on Rhodopou; it starts and finishes in the very pleasant square in Rodopos village. All the locals collect here to pass the time of day and watch the world go by. A great deal of this walk is waymarked and, as very few trees obscure the route, it is not difficult to follow. The few trees, however, offer very little shade, so this is not a walk to be undertaken at the height of summer. Getting into the church of Agios Ioannis Gionis is not an essential part of the walk but, if you wish to do so, ask for the key in Rodopos.

The bus turns in the village square. To **start the walk**, leave the square on your right and take the road which leads out past a bust, which is also on the right, in a corner of the square. Leaving the village, the road takes you past a large church on the right. This church is a firm landmark when you return to the village from a different direction, at the end of the walk. Two to three minutes past the church, just as you leave Rodopos, pass another much smaller and very pretty church tucked back on the right.

Five minutes' walking will take you out of the village. Ten minutes later (**15min**), the road starts to bend, turning into motorable track as it goes up and away from the village, passing well-tended vineyards along the way. At **45min** into the walk, the track passes between two concrete pillars. Disregard the lesser track heading off right beyond them and continue straight on. Ten minutes later you can look back to the sea behind you; you can just see it to the right as well. Then the view is lost, as the track bends left and inland. After **1h** walking a track peels off

79

left; continue on the track you have been following and, in another five minutes, the sea will come into sight again over to the right. The track divides (**1h15min**), and there is a small signpost in the fork indicating (in Greek) the direction for Agios Ioannis Gionis (ΠΡΟΣ ΓΙΟΝΗΣ). Take the left fork; you will notice a waymark on the boulder on the left of the track. Almost immediately pass two wells on the right. Five minutes further on, the track bends to the right and forms a 'T', just where a path goes off left. Continue round to the right and then, where the track forks a minute further on, keep up and left.

The track soon runs out — in an open area where there is a building set down to the left. Walk straight ahead in the direction you have been heading. Then go right and find a waymark sign indicating a path leading to a low wall on which a metal shrine is bolted. Look over the wall and you will see, far down below, the dilapidated but attractively-sited church of Agios Ioannis Gionis, shown in the photograph opposite. Secluded by trees and surrounded by open grazing land, the church is protected from the sea beyond by a ridge. To the left, the end of the Gramvousa Peninsula (photograph pages 28-29) is visible, reaching out into the sea. Take the footpath to the left of the low wall

and wind slowly downhill. Within a couple of turns you pass the small model church shown on the left; it stands sentry on a rock. Thirty-five minutes of *careful* walking on the loose earth-and-rubble path will bring you to the flat area around Agios Ioannis Gionis. Carry on round to the left end of the church (**2h 15min**) — an obvious place to rest, in the welcome shade of a plane tree.

Leave the church by going back through the gate where you came in, and walk on straight ahead (due south); two metal WCs stand to the right of the route. Keep down on the flat ground and pass a knee-high, pale grey rock on the left, on which there is a strong waymark confirming that you are going in the right direction. The next waymark is on a wooden post. Then the path goes over a broken mesh fence and heads towards a ramshackle animal stockade. Some metres/yards beyond the stockade, it goes to the left of two trees. Further waymarking leads you to the left of a lone tree, just beyond which the path divides. Take the right fork. Twenty minutes after leaving the church, the sea will be in sight ahead, with Gramvousa in the distance. Continue to follow the waymarking, which is sometimes on trees. Just after you see the waymarking on one of a clump of trees, look left to find the waymarks continuing on stones.

The path heads to the left of the 'V', through which you see the sea and, 30 minutes from the church (**2h45min**), it takes you to the edge of a small ravine — at the bottom of which, beside the sea, sits the church of Agios Pavlos. The path bends left into the hillside and crosses the ravine. Before long it starts to go down the hillside and, 40 minutes from Agios Ioannis, when the path splits, keep uphill on the waymarked fork. Agios Pavlos stays in sight down on your right as you cross the hillside.

Some **3h15min** into the walk, an hour from Agios Ioannis, there is a waymark star on a boulder to the left, under a carob tree. Make the most of the shade. Five minutes later the path climbs and then levels out again, going higher above the sea. Just before a band of trees on the hillside ahead, you will be able to look straight down

The church of Agios Ioannis Gionis is below, almost hidden by trees. Open grazing land surrounds this attractively-sited church, which lies protected in a hollow.

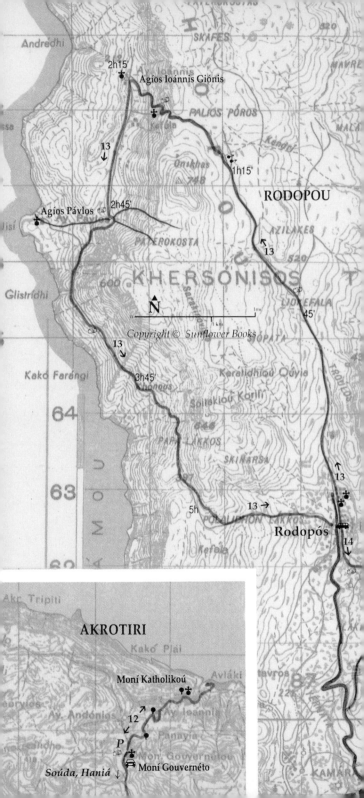

2h15'
Agios Ioánnis Giónis

PATEROKOSTAS
SKAFES   520
Andredhi   MAVRE

H   MALIA
PALIOS PÓROS
Kerála
13   Onákhas   Kengol
748   1h15'

RODOPOU

Agios Pávlos   2h45'
Ay. Pávlos   AZILAKES
Jisi   13   520
PATEROKOSTA

KHERSÓNISOS   T
600   LIOKEFALA
N   45'
Glistrídhi   1 km
Copyright © Sunflower Books
13
Kakó Farángi   Kerálidhlou Oúyia
3h45'   Spilakioú Korifí
Chonous   646

PARA LAKKOS
64   SKINARSA
397

63   13
13 →   13
5h   POLIMÍON LAKKOS   14
Kerála   Rodopós

62

Akr. Tripíti

AKROTIRI
Kakó Plái
Avláki
Moní Katholikoú
Ay. Ioánnis
Ay. Andónios   12
Panayía
P
Moní Gouvernéto
Soúda, Haniá ↓   Moní Gouvernéto

to the vivid blue sea on the right as it curls up on the rocky coastline below.

At **3h45min** (1h30min from Agios Ioannis Gionis) go through a stock control mesh gate and follow the path as it heads into the hillside and rounds a gulley. Ten to fifteen minutes later, the path wiggles upwards. Look ahead, across the hillside, and you will notice two footpaths crossing it — one somewhat higher than the other. The route back to Rodopos village is the higher one. It's a thirty-minute, gradual climb. Keep to the waymarking carefully on your climb, and look for an arrow at a division in the path, indicating the right-hand fork. Ten minutes on, a carob tree offers a little welcome shade. Fifteen minutes later, you are back on level ground, crossing a grazing area.

By **5h** (2h40min from Agios Ioannis Gionis), come to the end of the ridge on your left. Five minutes later, having crossed another, smaller grazing area, the path joins a rough track. Go left (there is an arrow on a rock); the track skirts a vineyard and, five minutes later, Rodopos is in sight straight ahead, with its easily-recognisable church. After **5h25min**, back on a concrete track, turn right at a junction (left is a very rough track) and head down into the village. In five minutes you will be back in the square.

14 THE RODOPOU PENINSULA:
RODOPOS • MONI GONIA • KOLIMBARI

Distance: 6km/3.7mi; 1h55min   **See map pages 82-83**
Grade: straightforward; track most of the way
Equipment: stout shoes, sunhat, picnic, water, suitable clothing for visit to the monastery (shorts are not allowed). **NB:** Moni Gonia is closed from 13.00-15.30.
How to get there: 🚌 to Rodopos (see Walk 13, page 79).
To return: 🚌 from Kolimbari to Hania (Timetables 7, 8). In addition, there are frequent buses between Kasteli and Hania.

This short but interesting foray into the Cretan countryside combines hillside and coastal villages, linking them with the quiet attraction of a seaside monastery. Starting in Rodopos, where life goes on around the arena of an ample village square, the walk goes through the smaller but very attractive village of Astratigos, past and through fields, up and down a valley, to the sea at Kolimbari, a relaxed backwater just off the main road within easy reach of Hania.

The bus turns round in Rodopos, which is also the starting point for Walk 13. **Start out** by walking back on the road (the way you came into the village). You'll come to house No 45 — the last house but one, before the road bends to the right. Here take the track leading off left. After you have turned onto it, you will see that it is signposted — on your left — to Astratigos (in Greek: ΠΡΩΣ ΑΣΤΡΑ–ΤΙΓΟ). Disregard the next turning left and keep straight on. Within a couple of minutes take the footpath that goes off and up left; it cuts a bend off the track. You'll rejoin the track at the top, by a shrine. Go straight over and down to the right and you will see the coast spread out below.

Soon, on a curve (the domed church shown in the drawing on page 12 will be ahead of you), bend right with the track. Then go left, onto another track leading directly to the church. Leaving the church on your left, head right and take the footpath. It becomes a narrow concrete track as it leads down through the village of Astratigos. When it forks (at a junction, where there is the corner of a concrete building and a fence running off to the left of it in front of you), go left past some vegetable patches. Continue, passing a pine tree on the left, until you meet the road. Turn right. At the end of the village you approach the back of a road sign. Here turn left onto a footpath which has a wall along its left side. Soon the path continues down between two walls. Half a minute on, disregard a path off left and continue straight on down, seawards.

Opposite: Follow the flowers to the sea and Moni Gonia.

84

The path goes down one side of a small ravine and up the other side. You begin your descent into this ravine at **25min**. Follow fencing round to the left; then continue, keeping the fencing to your left. Three minutes later, immediately past a curve, you will see a small gate ahead, off left. Just beyond here the path divides; head right. When the path next divides, within a couple of minutes, go right and cross over a streambed-that-was. Follow the uphill path on the far side. The next fork, where you head right, is overgrown and easily missed; watch out for it.

It's a four- to five-minute (often scratchy!) climb to the top. Here, **45min** into the walk, where the footpath meets rough track, you will see the sea again. Head right and continue until, several minutes later, the track joins another track, on a bend. Beyond here the track continues to the left of, and beneath some terraces. Soon (**1h05min**) strike off left towards the sea, by going through the netting fence on your left. (As you approach this fence, you will see the 'gate' in it; be sure to fasten the wires again.) Follow the rough track marks, which will be very grassy in early spring. The track divides when you have a rocky outcrop in front of you; go left and continue downhill. The route bends away from the sea then back towards it again. Eventually, the track turns into footpath — close to what must, at some time, have been a watercourse.

After walking for **1h20min** you will see the roofs and bell towers of the Gonia Monastery through the trees ahead. The last few yards/metres of footpath drop very steeply down to a wooden gate by the monastery. Leave the gate as you find it. There is a lovely view out to sea behind the monastery and, if you have the correct attire with you, it's worth wandering round inside.

After your visit, continue on to Kolimbari, five minutes away, along the road to the right. 'Mylos', just beyond the small harbour, is a pleasant place to stop for a drink. To pick up the Hania bus, walk through the village, keeping left at the post office (yellow and black signs). Walk along the last stretch of road — pleasantly shaded by tamarisk trees — and, at the crossroads, go diagonally opposite. The bus stops by the sign to Deliana and Hania, opposite the Hotel Rosmarie. (The proprietor of the hotel played a highly active part during the Second World War. His brave efforts are catalogued in framed newspaper cuttings displayed in the hotel. 'Rosmarie' was his code name.)

Walk 15 and Picnic 15: A fine view over the hills towards Sirikari — with a century plant (American aloe, see also page 2) in the foreground.

15 SIRIKARI TO POLIRINIA

Distance: 9km/5.5mi; 2h40min   **See photograph opposite**

Grade: moderate (steep descent, followed by easy gorge walk)

Equipment: stout shoes, sunhat, picnic, water

How to get there: 🚌 to Kasteli (Timetable 8): departs Hania 12.00; journey takes 1h20min. Change to Sirikari-🚌: departs 14.00; journey takes 1h15min (*sit on the right-hand side of the bus* for best views).

To return: Taxi from Polirinia to Kasteli (organise this before you leave Kasteli — telephone 22225), then 🚌 from Kasteli to Hania (Timetable 8): departs 19.00 daily; journey takes 1h20min.

The gorge leading to Polirinia is wide, pretty and peaceful in the extreme — filled with bright yellow Jerusalem sage in spring and crisp pink and white oleander in summer. And a bonus to this delightful walk is a visit to Kasteli, a very pleasant town where the local people are particularly charming and helpful. Taking the noon bus from Hania gives you time to wander round Kasteli, before catching your onward bus to Sirikari — a journey affording splendid views, as you bump slowly along into the heart of the countryside.

Get off the bus where it turns round at the end of its route, within sight of a solitary church. **Start out** by walking towards the church on a track. Just before reaching the church, go left on a grassier track. After a few paces, take the waymarked footpath off left) — a very pretty route, through trees and flowers. After **5min**, take the overgrown footpath branching left; it heads more steeply downhill. Although very overgrown, it is easily seen. Five minutes later, it is necessary to scramble steeply down to continue on the path. Having done that, *carefully,* follow the path. In a couple of minutes it leads you across a terrace and down onto a track. From here you can see a single house down below you, on the far side of the valley. It's a good landmark, as the path runs onwards just in front of it.

Cross straight over the track, looking carefully for the footpath which leads on down and round to the left. Very soon the path forks; go right, following the waymarking (which you will see about ten paces from the fork). Within a couple of minutes, the path divides again — either side of a bush. Go right again. Turn left at the next fork (where there are telephone wires close overhead). Carry on across a watercourse and then the riverbed just beyond it. The riverbed will become the gorge that this walk follows. Walk up the other side and, where the path comes to a 'T', turn right. Approach the house that we identified from the distance. Walk directly ahead, just to the right of this house, on what is a very overgrown bit of track. It turns into a footpath almost immediately and, in about a minute, at a heap of stones, heads up left; look for the waymarking. Soon go through a stock control gate, closing it carefully behind you. The path leads back down to the riverbed, which is lined with leafy plane trees, and before long passes a small ramshackle bridge off right. By now the route is within the beginnings of the gorge, and the air is light and fresh. The route cuts an arm off the riverbed, then continues along the left-hand side of it. Head on towards the water troughs and, just before them, cross the river bed diagonally and go up onto the far bank. Half an hour beyond the house (**1h15min**), go through another stock control gate. In **1h30min** the path has taken you well up to the right of the gorge, and the landscape has opened out. This is a good place to get your bearings.

Twenty minutes later, as you round a bend, you will see the village of Polirinia ahead in the distance, its church set on the heights. Follow the path as it bends to the right, away from the gorge, and then left again, to lead to the village. The river bed is now on your right. Cross a pretty, old cobbled bridge and, when the path forks just beyond the bridge, keep left. There is fencing on the right.

By **2h05min** from the start of the walk, go through one more mesh stock control gate and then continue on a broader, even path, which soon joins a track. Keep ahead

and, after **2h15min**, when a track comes in from the right, keep straight on and upwards. Four minutes later pass the first houses of Polirinia. This is a pleasant setting for a countryside picnic; see photograph page 86. Five minutes beyond the houses (you will be rounding a right-hand bend which has a rock on the right consisting of hundreds of slate-like layers), look for a steep narrow path — also on your right — that curves up right. (A large olive tree is on the left.) Three to four minutes up this path (which soon becomes cobbled), you'll come to a paved square with a water trough and a tree in its centre. Here head up left between the houses. Keep straight on; don't take the steps to the right, but follow the telephone poles. At the top, turn left and stay on the track. Come to the village *cafencion*, where the bus turns round (and a taxi could meet you).

16 KATSAMATADOS • MOURI • VOULGARO

Distance: 13km/8mi; 3h45min   **See map page 89**

Grade: moderate, with some downhill scrambling through a ravine

Equipment: stout shoes, sunhat, picnic, water

How to get there: 🚌 to Kasteli (Timetable 8): departs Hania 06.00, 07.15, 08.30, 10.00, 11.00, 12.00; journey takes 1h20min. Change to Katsamatados-🚐: departs Kasteli 12.30 or 14.00; journey takes 40 minutes. (*Note:* a taxi journey from Kasteli to Katsamatados is not expensive.)

To return: Take a taxi or the 🚌 (departs 17.10) going through Voulgaro to Kaloudiana on the main north coast road. At Kaloudiana you can pick up a Hania-bound bus coming from Kasteli (Timetable 8) at approximately 14.00, 15.30, 16.15, 17.30, 19.00. Taxi rank telephone numbers: Topolia (0822) 51259; Kaloudiana (0822) 31500

A fine wedge of western Crete's countryside — some lovely and varied landscapes — are covered in this walk. We take you through a gorge, along a pretty chestnut tree-lined valley, into some sweeping open countryside, and finally down a ravine well used by grazing flocks of sheep and goats. There's some scrambling en route, but for the most part the walk is on well-defined track.

If you take a taxi from Kasteli, the driver will stop for you to look down into the Topolia Gorge before dropping you on the outskirts of Katsamatados; otherwise you can see its walls quite well from the bus. If travelling by bus, ask to be dropped off about 350m/yds beyond the approach sign for the village of Katsamatados. (The village sign clearly says 'Kou<u>tsou</u>matados', but the villagers are adamant that this is a new-fangled and ugly name, so we have obliged them.) Here, not far past a *cafeneion* with a shady terrace opposite it, a concrete track leads down into the village.

Start the walk by leaving the main road on this track. Go down over a bridge and into the heart of Katsamatados. At a minor junction, leave another *cafeneion* off to the right and the rest of the village off to the left. Go straight ahead, over a water channel, onto a rough track. Pass a pretty church on the left and walk on — over another bridge and uphill slightly — along a very pleasant, shady track. Plane trees and chestnuts, olives and oleander keep everything cool, growing as they do along the water-course on the left. Anywhere along here is pleasant for picnicking. We are in the valley shown in the centre of the photograph opposite, a lush green setting. Cross another small bridge and then fork left (**10min**), keeping the water on your left. The track looks much like footpath because it's overgrown in places; vehicles used to be able to use it, until major work was carried out to provide mains water pipes. Now the surface is completely ruined. Soon the route crosses and recrosses what is now a dry streambed. Some **20min** from the village, go through double mesh stock control gates, closing them carefully behind you — if that's how you found them. The track starts to climb. Five minutes later, follow it as it bends sharply left and uphill. Disregard the remains of the footpath which continues along the route you've followed until now.

You will walk out of the shade as the track becomes much wider, leading through open countryside, with gentle green hills all round. Pass a stone shelter to the left and then half a dozen wooden feeding troughs. Go through a break in a mesh fence the far side of the troughs. It's a half-hour uphill walk to the top. There are wonderful views from here, as you can see in the photograph below. From here, go through the stock control gate, head down onto the track beyond it and turn left (**50min**); the right-hand fork leads to Sasalos (Walk 17). A few minutes along the route we can see down into Sasalos, below on the right.

Eight minutes past the view over Sasalos, the track turns away to the left, passing a field of vines on the left. In five minutes you will be facing a mesh fence, on the other side of which is a narrow streambed. On the far bank, beyond the bushes, is the church of Agios Athanasios. If you find it

Walk 16. We've climbed high enough now to look back to the village of Katsama-tados, seen below in the valley. Walk 17 enjoys this same view on the descent to Katsamatados and Topolia.

difficult to get into the streambed at this point, look for easier access over to your right.

Once in the streambed (**1h15min**) head north-northeast along it; a rough path leads you beside, in, and over the dry watercourse. Goats and sheep wander about and sit in the shade, close to the piped water running along the route. The streambed becomes a ravine a bit further on, where the animals shelter from the sun. Walking here in spring and early summer you'll find a mass of pungent dragon lilies standing sentry, together with thick Jerusalem sage. After about **1h30min**, you will come to a point where you can see through high, sloping rock walls to the countryside beyond. The route then starts to descend steeply, as streambed becomes ravine. You will have to scramble in places. Keep to the left-hand side and, five minutes later, at the narrowest point, a stock control fence bars the way; negotiate it and continue on downwards — picking your own route. The 'path' disappears for a while. After three minutes of clambering descent, look carefully, and you will see the overgrown footpath starting again to your right, just where the ravine's left wall falls away.

Some **2h05min** from the start of the walk, you will be able to see the sea over to the left of the Rodopou Peninsula. The path runs down and onto a track which crosses the watercourse. Head left. In early summer you will be surrounded by lovely bright yellow broom; in autumn the yellows and golds of vine fields lend mellow overtones to the scenery. Soon, go through a stock control gate and, after a minute — at the following junction — go straight across and then round to the left.

When the track you are on joins another on a bend (**2h30min**), walk downhill to the right. Within a few minutes, you will pass the first houses of Mouri, a very small village. Before long pass an old *cafeneion* on the right of the track; it has a black and yellow post box by the door, and vines and mulberries providing shade in front of it. As you leave the village, disregard a track going up left. About 45 minutes from Mouri, Voulgaro comes into sight. Thirteen minutes further on, the village of Topolia, with the gorge to the left, is also in view. You can't go wrong now, so head into Voulgaro, following the track as it bends right, round a church. When you are nearly there, the track goes over a bridge and becomes asphalt. At the main road, turn right into the village. There is a *cafeneion* on the left where you could arrange for a taxi; otherwise go on to the bus stop on the right-hand side of the road.

17 SASALOS • KATSAMATADOS • TOPOLIA

See map page 89; see also photograph page 91

Distance: 8km/5mi; 2h15min   **Grade:** easy

Equipment: stout shoes, sunhat, picnic, water

How to get there: 🚌 to Kasteli (Timetable 8): departs Hania 10.00, 11.00, 12.00; journey takes 1h20min. Change to Sasalos-🚌: departs 14.00; journey takes approximately 1h.

To return: 🚌 from Topolia to Kasteli (not in the timetables): departs Topolia 17.00; journey takes 30min (or taxi from Topolia to Kasteli). Change to Hania-🚌 (Timetable 8): departs Kasteli 17.30, 19.00; journey takes 1h15min.

Short walk: Sasalos to Katsamatados (5km/3mi; 1h35min; easy). To return, hail a taxi on the main road outside Katsamatados or call for one from the *cafeneion* on the main road.

Taking a straightforward route from Sasalos to Topolia, this walk makes a delightful afternoon's ramble. The countryside stays green throughout the season, oleanders cover the hillsides in early summer, and leafy chestnut trees line and shade the country track for part of the way. The walk carries you through a very pleasant stretch of Cretan countryside. Give yourselves plenty of time to wander around delightful Kasteli before taking the onward bus to Sasalos.

No matter where the bus stops, **start out** by walking on into the village, passing a sign indicating 'Floria' to the left. Then go right, over a bridge and, just past a building on the right, turn right on an earthen track. Walk past an old barn-like building set back from the road and head towards the church shown below. At the church, turn right along the

Walk 17: Before setting out, do have a quick look at this pretty blue-domed church in the village of Sasalos.

watercourse and follow the track through the trees — until you meet another track coming from the village. Join this track and head left uphill.

Eventually, the track levels out (**40min**). You can see the track to Voulgaro (Walk 16) — a long bend to the right — ahead. Look for a short, steep stretch of track heading left and sharply back. Follow it. Go through the stock control gate at the top and you will find yourself looking down from the ridge — with views over the fertile hills spreading out ahead into the distance (photograph page 91). The track bends down to a valley which leads to Katsamatados; you can see the houses below.

Walk down the track; 25 minutes from the top of the ridge, beyond half a dozen feeding troughs and a stone animal shelter on the right, the track enters the tree line. Follow it as it turns right and heads gently downhill beside the watercourse on your right. Continue on straight down this pleasant route, shaded by leafy chestnuts. The track's surface has been destroyed by the laying of water pipes and in places seems more like a footpath. Just before entering the village (where the Short walk ends), you will pass a small, very pretty church to the right. Walk over a water runnel, leave a *cafeneion* to the left and the rest of the village off to the right. Go straight ahead.

Cross over the riverbed and bend left with the concrete track, up onto the main asphalted road. Turn right here and continue towards Topolia (40 minutes away). Some 350m from the junction there is a *cafeneion* on your left, just past a bend. If you wish to end the walk here, have a rest and either wait for a taxi to pass or telephone for one.

Alternatively, keep walking, and soon you will see a tunnel cutting into the Topolia Gorge wall. Just before the tunnel entrance, an old sign written in Greek indicates Agia Sophia (Αγ. Σοφια). This is a church built inside a cave; it's just a short climb off the road. You can see a star at the mouth of the cave; it's just visible from the road. Having made the effort to climb up ... or not, continue along the main road, negotiating the short tunnel carefully. It's not very long; in fact you can see light at the far end of it. The Gorge of Topolia runs deep to the right of the road.

When you arrive at Topolia (**2h15min**), either wait for the bus or hail a passing taxi. There are usually taxis parked somewhere on the main road in this top part of the village.

18 SOUGIA • LISOS • PALEOHORA

Distance: 17km/10.5mi; 4h45min   **See Stop Press page 136**

Grade: moderate to strenuous

Equipment: stout shoes, sunhat, long socks/trousers, picnic, water

How to get there: 🚌 to Sougia (Timetable 6): departs Hania 09.00, 13.30; journey takes 1h30min.

To return: 🚌 from Paleohora to Hania (Timetable 5): departs 15.30, 17.00; journey takes 2 hours

Note: This walk is done more easily with an overnight at either Sougia or Paleohora. The current bus scheduling is quite tight, and it's a pity to rush through this walk.

Short walk: Sougia — Lisos — Sougia (9km/5.5mi; 2h30min; moderate). Buses depart Sougia for Hania at 07.00, 14.30 (Timetable 6).

The bus ride to Sougia, where this walk starts, is through a picturesque wooded valley and tree-clad hillsides — the western foothills of the White Mountains — glorious in autumn colours. The bus follows the Agia Irini gorge and riverbed down to the Libyan Sea. This sea is ever in view throughout the walk, which parallels the coast. The first stage takes you through an exceedingly pretty gorge, then uphill, over, and down to the ancient Roman site at Lisos, set back from the sheltered bay of Agios Kyrkos. The second pull brings us up and across a large, flat-topped headland, before we head back down to the sea and along a length of coast stretching all the way to Paleohora and punctuated by bays. If you don't stay overnight in Sougia, it's necessary to keep a wary eye on the time during this walk, otherwise you risk missing the late afternoon bus back to Hania and the north coast.

The bus will drop you beside the sea in the pleasant backwater that is Sougia. A sweep of shingle beach

High above Lisos we cross a plateau covered with spiny broom and spurge, before descending to Paleohora on the coast.

stretches out in front of you. **Start off** by heading right, on asphalt, past a pension/taverna; the sea will be on your left. Within a couple of minutes the road turns into track. Keep round to the right when the track divides at Sougia's small harbour. A rock face rears up in front of you, and an old sign points right, in the direction of Lisos. The path is waymarked and leads us into a very pretty gorge, thick with brilliant pink oleander in late spring and summer. There are ideal picnic spots all along this gorge, as you can see from the photograph on page 99. Choose your spot — under carobs, olives or pines, in the gorge or beside it.

Just **25min** into the walk, the smooth gorge walls tower up above you. Five minutes later, look up left: the path which you must follow leaves the gorge. Look for a boulder with a small bush growing out of the top of it; the route is waymarked. (If you come to a block in the gorge you have gone some metres/yards *past* the spot where the path heads upwards.)

Follow the path as it bends up and away from the gorge; at times it doubles back on itself. Another sign soon directs you towards Lisos again. It's just a seven-minute climb to a flat area on the hilltop, which you reach **40min** from leaving Sougia. Follow the path across the flat. The coast comes into sight again, to the left (**52min**). A minute further on, you will see Lisos below you, set back from its lovely sheltered bay. It's worth identifying the onward route from Lisos at this point. Look at the scene in front of you: over to the right is a ravine going down towards Lisos; to the left — looking carefully — you will see a definite cleft in the hillside. The onward path leads from Lisos up the hillside on the right-hand side of that cleft.

Continuing down to the site at Lisos, trace the way-marked path as it twists downhill; you may need to bend and twist round bushes in places. Pass the mouth of a cave (**1h**) set up on the right of the path. Follow the waymarking

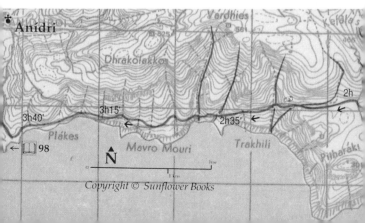

you an excellent view of the refuge high up at Kallergi, on the opposite side of the Samaria Gorge (see photograph on page 103). Notice from here two paths in particular: one in the foreground comes down to Xiloskala (Walk 20); the other, in the middle distance (to the right of Kallergi) leads through the conservation area into the Samaria Gorge.

Our path now takes us under a huge rock arch (**50min**); Cretan ebony hangs gracefully from it, and you cannot fail to feel as though you're in the very heart of the mountains here. There are massive, dramatic rock faces, peaks, boulders and formations all around, as the photograph below shows.

Dramatic rock formations characterise the exhilarating hike to Gingilos. See cover and page 103 for other photos of this awe-inspiring peak.

At **1h** into the walk, round a very large rock on the right; you will notice the shallow cave beneath it. Five minutes later, the route leads to the Linoseli Spring, where a water tank is tucked into the rock. The path goes on and up to the right, towards the massive scree slope shown on page 101, and a very obvious peak beyond pointing up into the sky. After the first bend, pick up a waymarked route which zigzags on up the mountain. Parts of it are on a firm scree base and there are cairns en route as well. Eighteen minutes past the Linoseli Spring, the path flattens out for a short distance. A large rock offers some shade.

Eventually (**1h40min**), you will reach a distinct ridge, the Linoseli Col. Here it may well be very windy indeed, but the thrill of being up so high and seeing for miles and miles is terrific. On a clear day, looking back to Kallergi, you might just be able to pick out Theodorou Island to the left of the refuge, off the distant north coast.

The Alternative walk returns from this col to Xiloskala via the same route, but for serious mountain walkers the climb to the top starts from this ridge. Look left to find an arrow pointing up the edge of the mountain. Follow the waymarking — do not lose sight of it — and it will lead you steeply upwards. In places it is necessary to clamber and scramble; you *need to be very surefooted and confident.* **Caution:** After about 2-300m/yds there is a hole almost 25m (80ft) deep just beneath the marked path — it's about 2.5m (8ft) in diameter, and completely vertical. *Beware!* Before long you will have a simply splendid view over the Omalos again and, by **2h25min**, the route will become easier as you near the top. Five minutes later, you will reach a cairn on a flattened area that *feels* like the top. In fact, the very highest point (Volakias) is thirty minutes distant. Press on if you feel the urge — we did *not,* because the way is not marked.

When you have taken in the tremendous view, make your way back to the ridge by following carefully the waymarking from the first cairn on the flat. It offers a choice of route, some ways easier than others. Use your discretion, knowing where you are heading. Fifty minutes later you will be back at Linoseli. It's pleasant, on the way down, to be able to pay more attention to the spectacular landscape and the trees — among them the pretty Montpelier maple. The descent back to Xiloskala takes about 2h30min. Make sure, if you sit on the resthouse terrace having a drink, that you are ready to jump on the bus, as it arrives, turns round and leaves almost immediately.

Distance: 8km/5mi; 2h

Grade: easy track walking for most of the way

Equipment: stout shoes, sunhat, picnic, water, torch (if staying overnight at Kallergi). An overnight stay at the Kallergi refuge can be arranged by telephoning 0821-20030/24647.

How to get there: 🚌 to Omalos (Timetable 3): departs Hania 06.15, 08.30, 16.30; journey takes 1h20min.

To return: Omalos- 🚌 back to Hania (Timetable 3): departures at 07.30, 10.00, 18.00.

K allergi is the mountain refuge in the Levka Ori (White Mountains) that hikers and climbers use as a base for exploring the range, under the guidance and supervision of the refuge's professional Austrian management.

However, you don't have to be an expert to enjoy its spectacular position, perched like an eyrie at 1677m/ 5510ft above sea level. The refuge provides an authentic retreat from the noisy world we live in and offers either basic or more pampered living accommodation and facilities.

This walk shows you the route to Kallergi, where you can have an evening meal and spend a night — by prior arrangement — or simply visit to marvel at the views, enjoy a picnic and revel in the peaceful atmosphere of the mountains.

Get off the bus at the end of its route, where it turns round in the car park at the top of the Samaria Gorge. Walk to the wooden railings by the viewpoint overlooking the gorge and look to the left of the gorge entrance. You will see a stone bench, set against a wall beneath a large conifer. **Start off** on the path leading away from behind

The Kallergi refuge sits perched atop a peak, in line with Gingilos; between these peaks, the Samaria Gorge slices its way to the sea.

this tree. It crosses the hillside, climbing very gradually at first and running almost parallel to the car park below. It passes a collection of conifers (**4min**) and then climbs more steadily, beginning to turn away from the road.

The path splits three ways (**8min**); keep to the left-hand fork. This climbs quite steeply and then leads round the head of a shallow ravine down to the left (**15min**). Look back across the car park and beyond the Tourist Pavilion, to Gingilos, the impressive grey landmass in the background. (Walk 19 climbs Gingilos; you can see the footpath zig-zagging up the opposite hillside.)

As the path which you are on rounds the shoulder of the

hill, the Omalos comes into view, spread out like a tablecloth far below. Continue on the path until it meets track on a hairpin bend (**25min**). A small cairn marks the junction; this waymarker is a help on the return journey. Head to the right up the rough track. Half an hour later you will reach the top. There is a shrine and an igloo-shaped stone shepherds' shelter here, bearing a plaque that commemorates bravery during the Second World War.

Our track divides at this shelter; take the right-hand fork and walk a further 150m/yds to the refuge — Kallergi — that you can now see clearly ahead, reached in **1h**.

The return journey follows the same route.

21 KALLERGI • MAVRI • MELINDAOU • KALLERGI

Distance: 16km/10mi; 5h35min   See map pages 104-105

Grade: for experienced mountain walkers

Equipment: walking boots, anorak, sunhat, headscarf, compass, picnic, water

How to get there: See under Walk 20. You will first have to walk from Xiloskala to Kallergi (1h). Alternatively, you can drive up to Kallergi if you have a four-wheel drive vehicle. An overnight at the Kallergi refuge can be arranged. See Walk 20 or 'Where to stay', page 42.

To return: Walk down to Xiloskala; then bus to Hania (see Walk 20).

A breathtaking hike in more ways than one, the trek to Melindaou is, without doubt, worth the effort involved. The lure of the high mountains is a compelling experience, and this walk — in the heart of the splendid Levka Ori (White Mountains) — is an exciting introduction to high mountain walking on Crete.

This expedition requires stamina, the ability to use a compass competently, and surefootedness. The rewards are ample, and walking in this area, we are sure, will mean the beginning of a long association with Crete's mountains. You will carry the views with you forever — the space, the fold upon fold of rock and mountainside, the colours and textures, the height, depth and strength of western Crete.

Having checked in at Kallergi, the mountain refuge, be sure to tell someone where you are going. Then **set off** — walk the length of the refuge and follow the short path leading to a track. This track heads off in an easterly direction, towards the mountains. You will follow it to 'Poria', the Shepherds' Saddle. The route affords a wonderful view of Kallergi and Gingilos; see photograph on page 103.

Some **20min** from Kallergi, when the hut is completely out of sight, and the valley falls away to the left of the track, you will have a wonderful view of mountains — and still more mountains. From here, on a clear day, it is possible to see all the way to Theodorou Island off the north coast (west of Hania, opposite Agia Marina).

By **45min** from Kallergi, rounding a bend in the track, you will be at the Shepherds' Saddle or 'Poria', as it is known by the shepherds themselves. Paths lead from here in different directions. Before going down towards the open area to the right of the track, look further ahead to see the shepherds' dwellings on the left. At the end of this walk, you will come down off the mountainside opposite these dwellings.

Then continue: turn right off the track and head across

The walker is a mere dot in the landscape on this high mountain walk which circles Mavri (the central peak). Melindaou is to the right.

the centre of the open area on a path, making for a stone igloo-shaped structure (with jagged rocks in the distance beyond it). Gingilos is just visible behind the jagged fringe. Pass the stone shelter and then look carefully for the first left turn. It bends back away from the view to Kallergi and takes you across the hillside. A slight knoll is seen on the highest point ahead of you. You are heading east. Seven minutes later, continue in an easterly direction, leaving a huge square boulder off to the left. Waymarking starts around here, and you *must be sure to find it* before embarking on the climb, which becomes very steep. To check that you are on the right route, look back to Kallergi some 20 minutes into the climb. You will see a blasted tree trunk. It is a striking sight against the hillside.

After **1h30min** — the last half of which involves a very steep climb — the route flattens out briefly; you will be level with the refuge, now far away in the distance. This respite doesn't last long, however, and the route continues on and up, beyond a substantial cairn. Fifteen minutes later, reach the top of the first ridge, from where you can feast your eyes upon yet more splendid mountains and the inspiring Cretan landscape.

Head left along the ridge in a northeasterly direction and follow the waymarking carefully, as there isn't a path to speak of. Within a short distance find the first of several cairns. Continue along the ridge. By **2h10min** you'll start climbing again. Follow the waymarking assiduously. Ten minutes later come to a short concrete pillar, with three bits of iron protruding from it. It has been placed here, together with a stick, as a sort of waymark. From this point you can see the route leading on across another ridge towards Mavri (the photograph above was taken here and shows the route clearly). Keep going; thirteen minutes later (**2h25min** into the walk), locate another cairn on the ridge. Go straight on up the ridge and, at **2h30min** (at the next cairn, near the top of Mavri), take the path curving round to the right across to the next slope.

At **2h40min**, having gone halfway along the ridge, look

for a path heading sharply *back left* round the other side of Mavri. This is the homeward route. You can either head back now or press on further and follow the path as it continues, skirting to the right of Melindaou's summit (see photograph caption on page 107).

There is no obvious point of return if you continue to Melindaou; the path leads on even further into the White Mountains, to Pahnes, the highest peak in the range — a couple of days' and nights' trek away. So unless you're with a guide, it's best to opt for the homeward path, identified after passing Mavri. It cuts a route lower down and back across the mountainside, in the direction of Kallergi. Follow the waymarking over a ridge and look down to the right, along the valley ahead. Spot a clear path running along the valley. Pick your way carefully down towards the path and the valley floor; it takes about fifteen minutes of rough going. Once on the floor of the valley, you'll pick up waymark arrows that will guide you back to the track just beyond Poria, the Shepherds' Saddle, where you started up the mountainside.

Should you be walking in April or May, the valley floor will be swathed in crocuses and lots of other lovely bright wildflowers — a heartening sight for the trek back to Kallergi. Well into the return journey, the path crosses a dried-up watercourse and continues unevenly all the way back to the track where the shepherds' dwellings stand as a landmark, 150m/yds from the Shepherds' Saddle. From here, retrace your steps back to the refuge; the sense of achievement is terrific.

Walk 22: In the height of summer this can look like a bridge to nowhere, without the torrents of spring coursing below it.

22 THE SAMARIA GORGE

See photographs on the cover, page 17, and opposite

Distance: 18km/11.3mi; 4-6h

Open: April/May-October (depending on rainfall)

Grade: strenuous, particularly if you are not used to walking, even though it's mostly downhill

Equipment: stout shoes or walking boots, sunhat, water bottle (in which to collect spring water), picnic, swimming things

How to get there: 🚌 to Omalos (Timetable 3): departs Hania 06.15, 08.30; journey takes 1h20min (get off at the last stop, Xiloskala). *To return:* ⛴ from Agia Roumeli to Hora Sfakion: departs Agia Roumeli 15.45, 16.30, 17.00, 17.45; journey takes 1h30min. Then 🚌 from Hora Sfakion to Hania (Timetable 4): departs 16.30, 18.30; journey takes 1h45min.

The Samaria Gorge may be one of the reasons why you have come to Crete. Even if it isn't, you will soon hear tell of it; few people can resist the lure of Europe's longest gorge. And you won't be disappointed. But although this walk follows a well-trodden path, walking the gorge requires some stamina and robust footwear is essential.

Enough about caution. Here's some scene-setting: the landscape is simply spectacular, from the top of the gorge at Omalos to the bottom at Agia Roumeli — and all along the south coast on your boat trip to Hora Sfakion (where you'll find your bus back to Hania and the north coast). The White Mountains tower around you as the route leads seawards under shady pine trees through which sunlight slants. You'll pass cool pools and cross wide-open stretches of ancient, bleached rocky riverbed. Imagine light and shadow; height and depth; rock in shades of grey, green, blue and brown; mountains, trees and sky; birdsong and silence. It's a special experience walking through this natural wonder. If you walk the gorge in springtime, the wild flowers are another bonus to the excursion. At whatever time of year you walk the gorge, don't go down helter-skelter, trying to beat any records. Go at a leisurely pace and take in your surroundings. We haven't given any times for reaching specific points on the walk for this very reason. Enjoy the day.

Important note: do not try to find an alternative route to the sea; *stay on the designated path through the gorge. This is imperative.* Swimming in the rock pools is forbidden; console yourself with the thought of a swim at the end of the walk.

The bus drops you by two *cafeneions* (with shops and WC), where you can re-organise yourselves before starting out. The **walk starts** on the 'xiloskala', the wooden staircase shown on the cover of the book. This is a well-devised, solid construction made of tree trunks. Before setting out, you will be given a ticket (no charge); hang on to it. Half of it will be taken from you at the end of the gorge; it helps wardens to ascertain if everyone has gone through the gorge at the end of the day and, of course, it aids 'statistics'. Doubtless there will be a mass of other people setting off with you, which isn't encouraging, but the crowd thins out as people establish their individual pace and walk and stop and walk again, marvelling at this splendid achievement of nature.

The first eye-catcher is Gingilos Mountain (see photographs on the cover and page 103) — a huge wall of rock towering majestically up to the right. You may well have already climbed Gingilos at our suggestion (Walk 19), before descending into the gorge; it's a tremendous feeling to see the mountain from here, particularly if you have been to the top ....

The staircase becomes a path and drops down a staggering 1000m/3280ft to the bottom of the upper gorge — in just the first two kilometres of the walk. There are springs and drinking troughs and a couple of WCs en route. Once you've passed the small chapel of Agios Nikolaos, nestling amongst pines and cypresses to the right, the route becomes less steep. When you reach the old hamlet of Samaria you will be about halfway to the sea. Lots of people make use of the benches and tables to enjoy a picnic here, although there are masses of other delightful and quiet spots within easy reach. One of the buildings (into which you can go and sign the visitors' book) has been restored for the wardens who replaced the original inhabitants when the gorge was designated a national park.

From Samaria, continue on towards the sea, past the Ossia Maria (Mary's Bones) Church. The path twists and turns in places, allowing for rock formation and geological contortion, crossing the watercourse by stepping-stones in some places. You will know when you reach the famous Sideroportes ('Iron Gates'), where the gorge is at its narrowest. The rock walls soar straight up about 600m/2000ft on either side of you, and the scenery opens out beyond this point. Be prepared to take your shoes off here and paddle across the Tarraios River (which is so full in winter that the gorge has to be closed).

There are ticket collectors and two refreshment/souvenir kiosks a couple of kilometres before you reach the

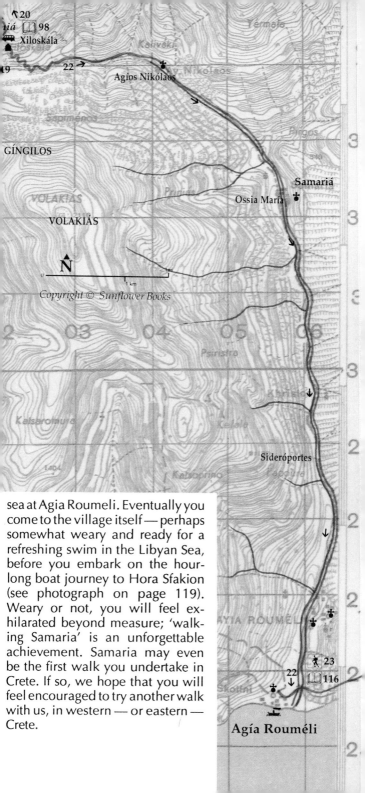

19

22 →

Agios Nikólaos · Kalíveki · NikÓlaos

Yermelo

GÍNGILOS

Pingos

Samariá ·

Ossía María ·

VOLAKIÁS

VOLAKIÁS

Ṉ

0   1 km

Copyright © Sunflower Books

2   03   04   05   06

Psiristra

Kalserotmure

Kaísoprino

Khristo ↓

Sideróportes
Papoura

↓

sea at Agia Roumeli. Eventually you come to the village itself — perhaps somewhat weary and ready for a refreshing swim in the Libyan Sea, before you embark on the hour-long boat journey to Hora Sfakion (see photograph on page 119). Weary or not, you will feel exhilarated beyond measure; 'walking Samaria' is an unforgettable achievement. Samaria may even be the first walk you undertake in Crete. If so, we hope that you will feel encouraged to try another walk with us, in western — or eastern — Crete.

AYIA ROUMÉLI · ·

🚶 23

22 ↓   📖 116

Skotíni

Agía Rouméli

23 AGIA ROUMELI TO LOUTRO

Distance: 15km/9.3mi; 4h35min   **See map pages 116-117**
Grade: moderate to strenuous, with some scrambling
Equipment: stout shoes, sunhat, picnic, water, swimming things
How to get there: 🚌 to Hora Sfakion (Timetable 4): departs Hania
08.30, 11.00; journey takes 1h45min. Then 🚢 to Agia Roumeli:
departs Hora Sfakion 09.30, 10.15, 11.00, 15.30, 17.00; journey takes
1h30min.
To return: 🚢 from Loutro to Hora Sfakion: departs 16.30, 17.45;
journey takes 30min. Then 🚌 from Hora Sfakion to Hania (Timetable
4): departs 16.30, 18.30; journey takes 1h45min.
Alternative walks: The energetic among you may wish to combine this
with walk 22 or 24 ... or even both.

The gorgeous sea walk from Agia Roumeli to Hora
Sfakion splits comfortably and conveniently into two
parts, and that's how we describe it. But whether you
undertake it as one walk or two, do start out early, to
benefit from the early morning cool and the sunrise.

The first stage of the walk has ample shade, but the leg
from Loutro to Hora Sfakion is virtually devoid of it. High
cliffs form a towering wall to the left, sometimes close at
hand, edging the path, in other places set back in high
majesty. Moving east, into the sunrise, you will skirt or
cross beaches, walk under pine trees — scrunching their
needles and inhaling the heady scent, edge along high,
but safe cliff paths, and scramble over boulders. With the
sparkling sea hemming your route on the right all the way,
you'll cover a great distance.

Agia Roumeli is a very pleasant, quiet place to stay
overnight, after the day's Samaria Gorge-walkers have left
with the last boat (17.30). The same goes for Loutro, where
there are also plenty of rooms to let. From the middle of
Agia Roumeli, **start out** by walking between the Samaria
Hotel and Tara Rooms for Rent — away from the sea and
towards the bottom of the Samaria Gorge. At the edge of
the village you will be on a rubble track. The track bends
round, away from the village. The riverbed leading from
the gorge is on your right.

Cross over the riverbed — via stepping stones between
an old bridge and the sea — picking up the waymarked
path on the other side. The sandy path then heads east
above the coast. Soon (**10min**) you will be walking along
the back of the next bay, one away from Agia Roumeli.
The path alternates between being sandy, rocky and stony
and runs 20m/yds to 50m/yds above the beach. When the
path descends to the beach (**22min**), follow it as it takes
you along another long beach (**35min**). Towards the end of

112

Take a break — or spend the night — at delightful Loutro.

this stretch, where a single rock sticks up out of the sea, the path heads uphill on sand, away from the beach. It is way-marked on a rock near the path. After crossing a stretch of sand, the path continues on rocks, up to the left.

Walking high now, enjoy the lovely smell of pines and the crunch of needles underfoot. There are fairly steep drops to the sea on the right in the high sections, but the path is so made that there is little fear of vertigo (**50min**). After **55min** walking, the route leads to a wooded area. Here cairns lead you into a left-hand curve— look for the waymarking — up and away from the sea. The route then curves right again and continues parallel to the sea, through pine trees. Ten minutes later, on sand again, cross along the top of a beach from where (**1h05min** from Agia Roumeli), the church of Agios Pavlos is well in view on the beach ahead. Keep up by the telephone poles.

Having walked down to visit the church — which is always open — return to the waymarked path, which continues above the church (**1h27min**). The path changes from sand back to stone and leads up through trees again. When it forks (**1h45min**), take the lower route waymarked to Loutro (in Greek: ΛΟΥΤΡΟ). Five minutes later pass a well. You're high over the sea (**2h05min**) on a cliff: goats graze on the hillsides, and more high cliffs rise left above you. The sea on your right shimmers in the rising sun, all sorts of shades of blue. By **3h30min** the path will start heading down to the sea once again, avoiding a gorge straight ahead. As it nears the sea, it forks. Look for a cairn to the left and the waymarking: it looks as if you have to take a dive into the gorge but, in fact, you will head down and across — onto a lovely small beach. Here there is

crystal-clear water, small sea caves and a miles-from-anywhere feeling.

Having relaxed for a while, continue on the path that brought you onto the beach. Go up the hillside on the other side of the gorge on a stony path that climbs quite gently. Ahead and below there is another small beach, with buildings on it. The path goes round high up on the cliff behind it, and here there is a chance that vertigo sufferers will find it a slightly testing experience, as the path is rough and goes quite near the cliff-edge. Twenty minutes from the swimming spot, the path needs some careful negotiation before heading down onto the next beach. Once onto it, walk along its length to the buildings and cross the concrete of both tavernas (you might feel it politic to have a drink en route …).

Go up the concrete steps (two flights) and head off behind the last building on the right. A rough-hewn path goes up above the tavernas. Before long, look straight ahead; to the right you will see cairns and waymarking leading up into the rocks above right. Head up. The village you can see up to the left is Livaniana. The path is waymarked with red and white splashes; where it forks, go right and then through a gate. The path forks: take the left-hand path upwards, towards the fence. From the corner of the fence, follow it down to where the route divides (at a sign, 'Café, Restaurant, Rooms'). Take the left-hand fork, picking up waymarking. It leads down to a group of mature carob and olive trees. Continue along the line of the hillside, dipping down with the path as it runs parallel with fenceposts — then picking up occasional waymarks leading to a 'Restaurant Phoenix' sign. Keep left and zigzag up towards the headland. As you reach the top of the rise, you will see a castle ahead on a flat open stretch of ground — in a very commanding position. The path curves round to the right, towards the castle, and then goes down, off to the left. There is a stunning view of the bay ahead and, as you round the first corner, the village of Loutro comes into view, fringed by the blue, blue sea.

Distance: 6km/3.7mi; 2h

Grade: strenuous, with some scrambling; **possibility of vertigo**

Equipment: stout shoes, sunhat, picnic, water, swimming things

How to get there: 🚌 to Hora Sfakion (Timetable 4): departs Hania 08.30, 11.00, 14.00; journey takes 1h45min. Then 🚢 to Loutro: 09.30, 10.15, 11.00, 15.30, 17.00; journey takes 30min.

To return: 🚌 from Hora Sfakion to Hania (Timetable 4): departs Hora Sfakion 07.00, 11.00, 16.30, 18.30; journey takes 1h45min.

Alternative walk: Although it would be long, you may like to combine this walk with Walk 23 — or even start at Xiloskala (see page 100, Samaria Gorge walk).

I f you approach Loutro from Walk 23, your path divides at a shrine; both routes lead into the village. Before descending, however, look out across the bay to the far hillside: you'll see your onward path leading all the way along it.

If you haven't stayed overnight here, or arrived this morning by boat, you will at least take a break here, perhaps for a swim or a meal at the waterside taverna shown on page 113. Then **start out** on Walk 24: leave Loutro by the eastern end of the village, just before a shuttered house with a gate (No 25). Turn up left behind some old buildings. A sign on a tree, 'Sfakia/Anopolis' and 'Beach', then directs you round left. Stones are waymarked. Follow the arrow on a stone pointing right, and go up towards another single old house. Reaching the house, go left and, beyond it, you will see the path going on across the hillside. Soon pass a shrine; the view is magnificent, down over and onto the sea on your right. Look back at Loutro and the castle above the village.

Some **15min** from Loutro, the path runs very near the cliff-edge, and there is a steep drop down to the sea, which might concern those who suffer from vertigo. Then, **30min** from Loutro, the path crosses a stretch of sand scree which might also unnerve vertigo sufferers. Ten minutes later, you'll be walking along the back of a beach.

At **50min** from Loutro, pass a church on the right and continue along the coastline. The magnificent sweep of

One hour east of Loutro you will come upon an inviting sweep of beach, set against a backdrop of awesome cliffs.

Copyright © *Sunflower Books*

beach shown in the photograph on the preceding page comes into view. Cross it in **1h**. There is little shade on this very exposed walk, and you might well find someone else in it — under the rocky overhang at the back of the beach. Having swum or not, time and inclination allowing, continue along the edge of the beach. At the far end, a small path leads off in an easterly direction. The route to Hora Sfakion now continues via coves and rough coastline; it's easy to lose the path, so do watch carefully for the cairns marking the way — which at times leads along the shore, over rocks and pebbles.

Just under **1h20min** from Loutro (about forty minutes short of Hora Sfakion), the path runs very high above the sea, across the mountainside. There is a sheer drop down to the right, and the path is only about 45cm/18in wide. It will be uncomfortable for vertigo sufferers for approximately 10-12 minutes. Eventually the path leads up to a bend in the main asphalt road leading into Hora Sfakion.

Turn right downhill and continue into Hora Sfakion (**2h**), where you can take a well-earned rest before the bus ride back to Hania. Hora Sfakion is shown on page 119.

25 IMBROS GORGE • KOMITADES • HORA SFAKION

See map page 121

Distance: 11km/6.7mi; 3h50min

Grade: fairly straightforward gorge walking

Equipment: stout shoes, sunhat, picnic, water, swimming things

How to get there: 🚌 to Imbros (Hora Sfakion bus, Timetable 4): departs Hania 08.30; journey takes 1h30min. *Hint:* Sit on the left-hand side of the bus.

To return: 🚌 from Hora Sfakion to Hania (Timetable 4: departs 16.30, 18.30; journey takes 1h45min.

Or shorten the walk by 4km: take 🚌 from Komitades to Hora Sfakion (Timetable 16): departs Komitades 15.30; journey takes 10 minutes. Change to Hania-🚌 (Timetable 4): departs 16.30, 18.30; journey takes 1h45min.

This is a really delightful amble through the peace and quiet of pines in the Imbros Gorge, which narrows and widens in places very dramatically — until you reach the south coast and the Libyan Sea. The bus rides are quite long, since you follow a winding route from the north to south coast and then back again, but these journeys enable you to see a good slice of Cretan countryside.

The bus will drop you in the village of Imbros. **Start out** by walking on, in the same direction as the bus is continuing. At the end of the village, just by a shrine on the left-hand side of the road, turn down hard left onto a track. This track leads away from the village and becomes a footpath as it meets the streambed. The stream — when it flowed — would have coursed its way to the sea from here, via the gorge. Once you are on the route, it's virtually impossible to lose your way.

Turn right and, very soon, you will be in the gorge itself, surrounded by Jerusalem sage, striking in spring and early summer. The route leads all the way to the coast; sometimes the path is in the gorge, sometimes it runs beside it to avoid large boulders. Anywhere around here is a good place to picnic; see the photograph below. Throughout this walk the path is easy to see, and you can pick your own route without too much difficulty. By **50min** into the walk, you will be briefly on a donkey trail. Five minutes

Here's a welcome opening in the (generally steep and narrow) Imbros Gorge — the setting for Picnic 25.

Hora Sfakion seen from the sea. There are regular sailings to Loutro, Agia Roumeli, Sougia and Paleohora.

later, a tree that has fallen across the route has to be negotiated. It's a good place to take a photograph, as you go round, over or under the huge trunk. After **1h30min** of easy walking you will pass an animal shelter and water trough. Keep on going down and along the gorge. At **2h20min** you can see the south coast and the sea ahead in the middle distance. You should just be able to make out the 14th-century Venetian fort, Frangokastello.

Jerusalem sage (Phlomis fruticosa); see also photograph page 30.

In **2h30min** the countryside has opened out and, looking to the right — quite carefully — you will see a faded waymark arrow by a stone wall-bordered path. Follow the path which will take you to the main road. The village off to the left is Vraskas. Step down onto the road and turn right. Walk on to the village ahead, Komitades.

You can either wait here for the bus (which comes through at about 15.30-16.00) or walk on to Hora Sfakion — an hour away. To continue to Hora Sfakion, keep on the road and, some ten minutes later (where you join the main Hora Sfakion road at a T-junction), turn left. You can wait for the Hania bus here but, if it is full, it may not stop. Some **3h50min** from the start of the walk, you will reach the centre of Hora Sfakion, its small harbour bristling with *cafeneions* and tavernas. There is a beach in the village from where you can swim.

119

26 ASKYFOU • ASFENDOS • AGIOS NEKTARIOS

Distance: 17km/10.5mi; 4h30min

Grade: moderate (straightforward, but fairly long)

Equipment: stout shoes, sunhat, picnic, water

How to get there: 🚌 to Kares (Hora Sfakion bus, Timetable 4): departs Hania 08.30; journey takes 1h15min.

To return: 🚌 from Agios Nektarios to Hora Sfakion (not in the timetables): departs 16.00 daily; journey takes 20 minutes. Change to Hania-🚌 (Timetable 4): departs 16.30, 18.30; journey takes 1h45min.

O ne of our favourite walks, this excursion combines a good bus ride, covering masses of ground, with a walk across the lovely plain at Askyfou and over some easy mountain terrain. We finish with a descent through a gorge, with the Libyan Sea as our goal. The road that the bus follows is the route that thousands of war-weary soldiers trudged along in 1941, when they withdrew — under relentless air attack — to the south coast. The walk leads you through a gorgeous chunk of Cretan countryside — spectacular anytime, but particularly picturesque in spring, when the plain at Askyfou is dotted with poppies (see next page) and the gorge is lined with bright yellow Jerusalem sage (see pages 30 and 119).

Be ready to get off the bus when, having wound up and round hillsides, you see the Askyfou plain come into sight below left. Before you leave the bus, it passes an eye-catching old Turkish fort, strategically positioned on a hillock mid-plain. Then the bus passes the sign denoting the boundary of Askyfou village. You will be dropped at a junction and the bus will go straight on. **Start out:** cross the road, take the turn left off the main road, and then head down towards a hamlet and the plain below it. At the next junction you will be in the hamlet of Kares; turn left onto a concrete track. The track forks (**10min**) by a telephone pole (there is a walnut tree on the corner); go off left. This route will take you across the plain itself, via fields of vegetables planted and tended by the Askyfou villagers. Within a few minutes, ignore a rough stone track going left (the track you are on also becomes stony). Pass a well, also on your left. Soon, at the next cross-tracks, turn left and head in the direction of the Turkish fort. By **20min** into the walk, meet an asphalt road: go left. A church, its graveyard surrounded by the customary cypress trees, lies to the left.

The road rises as you approach Seli, the next village, and a concrete track takes you round to the right. The track

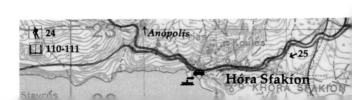

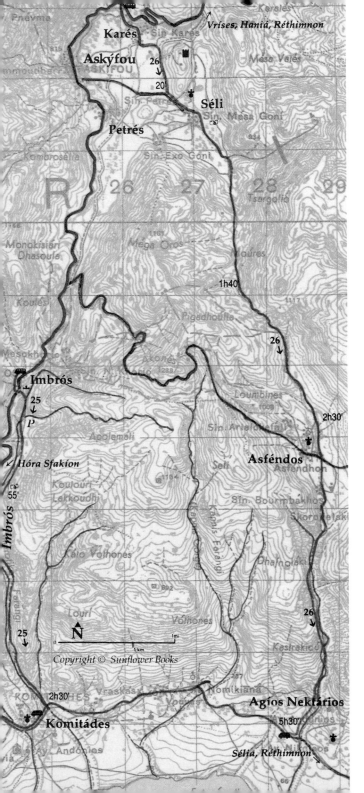

Vríses, Haniá, Réthimnon

Karés

Askýfou

26

20

Séli

Petrés

Sín. Mésa Goní

Sín. Exo Goní

R   26   27   28   29

Tsargoliá

Monakísiari
Dhasoúla

Mega Oros

Maúres

1h40'

Koulés

Pigadhoúlia

26

Mesokhó

Akónes

Imbrós

Loumbínes

25

P

2h30'

Sín. Arialokéfal

Hóra Sfakíon

Apolemáli

Seli

Asféndos

Asfendhon

55'

Kouloúri
Lakkoúdhi

Sín. Bourmbákhos

Skorovétaki

Imbrós

Kála Volhónes

Kamis Farangi

Dhafnoláki

Louri

Volhónes

26

N

Copyright © Sunflower Books

Keskakoú

25

Nomikiána

2h30'

Vraskastí

Agíos Nektários

Komitádes

5h30'

Ay. Andónios

Sélia, Réthimnon

skirts the village and ends by an old building with 'No. 20' painted on it and double metal doors. Take the earth track straight ahead, to the right of the building. Stay on the track as it bends round and away from Seli, with wonderful views (see below). Continue straight on, ignoring a grass track to the right and another to the left. Seli is directly behind you now. Just after a large low building on the left, go through a mesh gate and keep going until, 25 minutes later, the track runs out. Now, **1h** into the walk, just 20m/yds before the end of the track, look for a footpath on the right. It is waymarked with red paint. Head right on this waymarked path and start climbing. The path divides (**1h10min**) and an arrow directs you left; look up and see another waymark ahead. Stay with the waymarking; ten minutes later the path levels out as it reaches an open grassy area. After seven minutes the path divides; go left (red arrow). Ahead, on the hillside, you'll see some stone walls that underpin your ongoing path. Aiming for those walls, follow the path past a water trough and under two large hollyoak trees. Then the way leads up and right, towards a sycamore tree, before continuing on the stone-built section ahead. The footpath widens on the walls which zig-zag up to the top of the rise — a long way now from the plain below where you set out.

Now a well-established path gradually starts the descent to the sea. It obviously took a lot of work to create this path. Keep on going down; the route leads across

another open grassy area, past an animal shelter and a group of trees set off to the left. Reaching the far side of the flat grazing land, you will catch sight of the distant sea for the first time. Follow the path as it starts to head downwards again. *Do* keep the waymarks in sight, as there is occasionally a choice of footpath and, although the direction is fairly obvious, it is reassuring to use the waymarking. You'll pass a water trough (**2h20min**) on the left, and then, when the path divides, keep left. Notice a road running up on the hillside to your right; it's the Imbros/Asfendos route. At **2h25min** into the walk, keep left when the path forks. Be aware that you are heading for the 'V' of the gorge ahead of you. When the path splits again, keep right — always heading for that 'V'.

As you round a bend (**2h30min**) the very basic houses of Asfendos come into sight. The village church is high up above on the right. Three minutes later, the footpath ends as it joins a rubble track; turn left. Then, on the first bend (where there is a house/*cafeneion* on the left), take the rough track that leads right off the main track. It is still pointing in the direction of the 'V'. Leave Asfendos and take the rocky path that goes off left almost immediately. For seven minutes or so, there are walls either side of the path, which show evidence of past waymarking. Keep going straight down, disregarding paths off left or right, and make sure you have walls either side of you at first, and then on at least one side or the other. The 'V' becomes

a 'U' in the distance, the left-hand side of it opening outwards as you near the gorge. The path is thickly edged with Jerusalem sage; a glorious yellow-bright mass in spring. About half an hour from Asfendos, there are clear signs that part of this path was formerly paved. You can see the gorge clearly now, ahead of you. Forty minutes from Asfendos, you will see the sea in the cleft ahead, and scree comes in on the right. Five minutes further on, pass a huge waymarked boulder. The path

Looking westwards towards the White Mountains, from the poppy-bright plain of Askyfou (20 minutes into the walk).

then does a double-bend and curves down the hillside. Although you are high, the gorge is too layered to pose any problem for vertigo sufferers.

Before long you will be walking on the level for a while and, 55min from Asfendos (**3h25min** from the start of the walk), you will be able to see the beach and sea below and ahead of you. Ten minutes after spotting the beach, stay on the path that bends round to the left and snakes down the hill, disregarding a smaller path that leads across the side of the gorge. Your path curves round by a shepherds' hut with a metal door — built into the mountain — and, three minutes later, it passes across the bottom of an animal stockade. If you find any forks in the path, just continue in the same direction, down the side of the gorge. Before long, you will find that the route criss-crosses the dry riverbed. Ten minutes from the start of these riverbed crossings, you will be high above the dry bed again.

Some 1h50min from Asfendos (**4h20min**), the path divides. Go down left, as an orange arrow on a rock indicates. Fencing starts and, within a few paces, Agios Nektarios comes into sight below. Waymarking (which has been sporadic) leads you away from the fencing on your right. Soon the path becomes a track, and you will walk between the few houses of Agios Nektarios and onto the south coast road. A church lies to the left. Turn right on the main road and continue until you come — very shortly — to a *cafeneion* on the left (currently painted sludge green). A bus will pass at about 16.00; it's worth trying to hitch a lift to Hora Sfakion in the interim ....

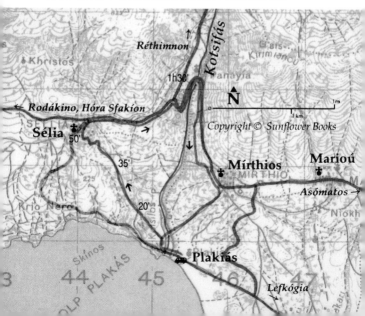

27 PLAKIAS • SELIA • THE KOTSIFAS GORGE • MIRTHIOS • PLAKIAS

See map opposite, photograph page 31 and Stop Press page 136

Distance: 9km/5.8mi; 3h

Grade: moderate to strenuous

Equipment: stout shoes, sunhat, picnic, water

How to get there: 🚌 to Rethimnon (Timetables 1, 2): departs Hania every half hour; journey takes 1h. Change to 🚌 from Rethimnon to Plakias (Timetable 15): departs 08.15, 09.30, 11.30, 13.45; journey takes 40min.

To return: 🚌 from Plakias to Rethimnon (Timetable 11): departs Plakias 09.30, 11.00, 12.45, 15.00, 19.15; journey takes 40min. Change to 🚌 from Rethimnon to Hania (Timetables 1, 2): departs every half hour; journey takes 1h.

T his walk, taking in a dramatic section of the south coast and featuring the Kotsifas Gorge, has good panoramic views of mountains and seascapes at every turn. We've included it for those staying nearby — pleasant as it is, it doesn't merit a special trip, if you're based elsewhere.

The bus will set you down by the Hotel Livicon in Plakias, near the small harbour full of fishing boats. **Start out** by walking towards the boats. Turn right before Zorba's Taverna, onto the hard-packed dirt track which twists through olive groves and carob trees. After a few minutes, ignore a track curving off right — this is your return route. After **20min** fork right and, in **28min**, keep up left. Plakias falls away behind you. It's a steep climb — you'll get up to nearly 330m/1000ft above sea level — but after some **30min** you can stop to admire the breathtaking vista over Plakias Bay (photograph page 31) and east towards the high peak of Kyrimianou. A minute later, the track divides; go left.

About **35min** above Plakias, you can see the houses of Selia above you — another ten minutes' climb away. In **38min** turn hard right, to climb steeply. Five minutes later, on a long bend to the right, go straight up off the corner onto a paved path. Plakias Bay is behind you. In under **50min** you reach Selia. Turn left into the village and then go right by the telephone pole. Pass the church on your left and curve right to join the main asphalt road. Continue straight on (do *not* go up left to Rodakino). Then follow the road as it curves to the left. To compensate for the asphalt underfoot, you have more breathtaking views over the Libyan Sea. Further along the road there are glimpses towards the gorge ahead, the steep hillsides and the river valley which tumbles down towards Plakias. On the western face above the road, on the highest slopes, are remnants of the cypress forests which once covered much of Crete. What remains at these heights is safely out of reach of even the most intrepid goat. Goats — and the Venetians, who prized the timber for their galleons — have been responsible for the loss of Crete's natural forests. On the eastern face you'll see terraces; in Venetian times these may have been planted with wheat.

You drop down to the foot of the Kotsifas Gorge in **1h30min**, just beyond the joining of the roads to Hora Sfakion, Rethimnon and Lefkogia. A modern road bridge has been built over what is, in winter, a raging torrent. Continue on the road, making for Mirthios. Ten minutes downhill you will see a track on your right, leading down into the valley. Either stay on the road, or use the track (it rejoins the road before Mirthios, after a short stiff climb). Soon after the village sign, come to a welcoming taverna on your right, with a terrace that boasts a fine view over Plakias Bay. Refreshed, walk a few metres (yards) further on, to a small car parking area. Take the concrete steps on the far side of the parking area down onto a goats' path that winds steeply down through olive groves. After two minutes you pass a trough with fresh water, and the path goes left, beside a water channel. After ten minutes or so, you come out into open countryside.

Now you have a choice of several routes back to Plakias. We'd suggest the more direct, steeper path which leads straight on and falls directly towards the village. *Go carefully.* The path finishes abruptly on a dirt road (which has wound down from Mirthios). Follow this road, heading left, for about 100m/yds. Then you'll spot a track at a right angle — just past what appears to be a new flat-roofed house. This track dives downhill to Plakias. On the way down, off to the east, a conical hill crowned by the remains of Plakias Castle, can be glimpsed. All that is left of this Venetian fortress are the yellowish chapel walls. (During the Second World War, the Germans also appreciated the strategic significance of the bay, and the cliffs to the east are honeycombed with tunnels and gun turrets.)

Twenty minutes downhill, at a T-junction, go down right. Then take a path off left at the next bend. The narrow path leads onto track, where you turn left. Beyond a building, turn right, and the track flattens out as you pass a camp site on your left. Cross a bamboo-shaded bridge and rejoin the road on which you set off. Turn left to return to the harbour (**3h**).

28 FOURFOURAS TO KORAKIA (IDA RANGE) AND RETURN

Distance: 14km/8.7mi; 5h20min

Grade: strenuous

Equipment: walking boots, anorak, sunhat, compass, picnic, water

How to get there: to Rethimnon (Timetable 1): departs Hania 05.30; journey takes 1h. Change to to Fourfouras (not in the timetables); this is the school bus, and it has the word ΜΑΔΑΡΕΣ (MADARES) on the front; journey takes 1h30min.

To return: from Fourfouras to Rethimnon: departs Fourfouras 14.30; journey takes 1h30min. Change to from Rethimnon to Hania (Timetable 1): departs 15.30, 16.15, 17.00, 17.30; journey takes 1h.

I t's hard to imagine grand Psiloritis and the beautiful Amari Valley playing major roles in the Second World War. But they did, being the backdrop for many daring, courageous Resistance efforts. This walk makes a good day's hike to a trig point, Korakia (or 'Kora-**char**', as the locals say), where you can survey the scene above and below, contemplate the present and imagine the past. It's an uphill climb in no uncertain terms, and the constraints of bus times mean that you have to keep moving. (It's worth considering a taxi ride back to Rethimnon to save rushing.) You will want to take your time — both because the area is historically interesting … and because the route is not always very obvious.

The bus stops by a petrol station on the outskirts of Fourfouras. Behind the village is Mount Kedros — a comfortable, rounded shape compared to the challenging mountainside we tackle on this hike. Take a look at those mountains in the background behind the petrol station and notice their jagged teeth, right of centre. Beyond their fringe, the slopes of Mount Ida (Psiloritis) change texture and colour. That's where we're going!

Start out by walking back in the direction the bus came.

After about 1h45min, come to some hollyoaks and take a welcome break. The path climbs above the crag ahead and continues ever up to Korakia.

Take the first track leading off right, heading in the direction of the mountains. At a fork, go right again. By **25min** walking from the road, you're at the start of the climb. (The track up to the start of the climb is only on a gradual incline.) Keep going until you pass a huge flat concreted area off to the left, which looks like the makings of a Greek football ground. Then, at a T-junction, turn right. The track then forks round to the left, and it may be necessary to negotiate a stock control gate (depending on what time of year it is, and what the shepherds are doing with their flocks). If there is a gate, leave it as you find it. Continue on towards the mountain, now not *quite* so out of reach. Follow the track when it bends firmly right and leave it within a short distance of the bend: here way-marking indicates a footpath leading off left, up a bank.

Start moving across and up the hillside, following the waymarking. The path meets the edge of the end of a ravine etched deep into the mountainside. You will see a distinct hollyoak tree standing on its own. The path you are on curves back on itself to the left, immediately beyond this tree (you may find a cairn waymarker). As you walk on uphill you will see water troughs over to the right. You can't miss one very distinct rock standing out en route, shaped like a large beast. Just beyond it there is a lovely panoramic view down over Fourfouras and across to Kedros. On a clear day it's possible to see Crete's south coast from up here, even though you have still got a fair

Convolvulus

Thorny burnet (Sarcopoterium spinosum)

Cretan Peony (Paeonia clusii)

climb to Korakia; imagine what the view will be like when you get there!

The path becomes narrow and very steep (**1h05min**), and soon you will notice an outcrop of rock on the left with three hollyoak trees on it. Beyond them you can see for miles over the Amari Valley. A few paces after this outcrop the path splits. Go right and up (the left-hand fork goes to a spring that is piped along this route).

Continue uphill, staying with the waymarking. About eighteen minutes later, as the path rounds a bend, there is a tree-lined cleft in the hillside — which is steep enough to cause a brief moment of anxiety to vertigo sufferers. The path almost immediately bends back left across the hillside away from the cleft, in a northeasterly direction. When it bends back in a northwesterly direction, head on up again — look for a waymark on the top of a step of rock (it's hard to find, because you won't see it until you are almost walking over it — Fourfouras is in a southwesterly direction from that mark).

The path comes to some hollyoak trees (**1h45min**) and the going is easier — not quite so steep. We're at the point shown in the photograph opposite. We'll pass the top of the craggy cleft (part of which we passed lower down), and then the waymarking will become directional — as opposed to marking an actual path. (In fact on the way down you will need to have noticed these clefts and bands of trees, as the waymarking is harder to follow.)

Ten minutes from the last bunch of hollyoaks, having walked through a stretch of more barren landscape, the path curves round a single hollyoak. A minute beyond it, look for a waymark on the trunk of a pine tree to the left of the path. Some **2h** from the start of the walk, you will be in another distinct wooded area of hollyoaks and pines that form a sheltered area for flocks. There's an outcrop of startling boulders in the middle of it, and some shepherds'

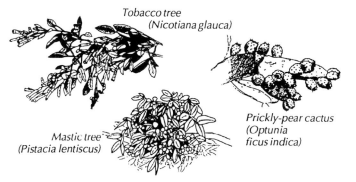

Tobacco tree
(Nicotiana glauca)

Prickly-pear cactus
(Optunia
ficus indica)

Mastic tree
(Pistacia lentiscus)

ruined dwellings. From the beginning of the band of trees notice a higher, sort of 'fence' of rock above you; then head off right. Look onwards from the old building's walls; there is a waymark between two hollyoak trees — nearer the one on the right. The path bends on up from here, and there is a dramatic ravine on the right-hand side of it. We are far above it. The path bends but goes straight up from the left end of the ravine.

Reaching another flatter, wooded and sheltered grazing area for flocks (**2h30min**), look uphill and pick up the route up again, beyond the trees to the right. There isn't any waymarking in the trees, so look carefully for the onward route. Once away from the trees, the way curves round a large blunted point of rock. As you round the corner from this particular rock 'obelisk', look up, and you will be able to see the ridge ahead, with its changing rock colour and texture quite clearly visible now. Remember, that's the level we are taking you to today.

As you continue up towards the ridge, look to the left of it; there's a huge thumb of rock standing alone. The path aims up roughly in that direction. To the left of the 'thumb', there's a smaller rock, and then another hump of rock. The route snakes up nearer those rocks (one of which looks like rabbits' ears when in closer proximity). Approach the 'ears', and you will find it marginally easier to continue by leaving them to your right — go to the far side of them — to get to the higher level.

It's not much further to the trig point and the wonderful view at the top of Korakia. There's a shepherds' stone shelter up here as well (**3h**). If you have planned to continue onwards, there is no defined path; just head across the grazing area and on up that huge hump of mountainside, leaving Korakia and the jagged rock teeth behind.

Heading back down to Fourfouras, watch the waymarking carefully. It's not as easy to keep to the path on the way down, and you musn't hang about if you intend catching the afternoon bus.

BUS TIMETABLES

The timetables given here are 'summer' timetables — valid for the height of the season. Buses are likely to be less frequent in spring and autumn. Be sure to collect an up-to-date timetable from the bus station before setting out on any excursion. *Note:* Express buses are unlikely to stop at intermediate destinations. See Index to locate quickly timetable number for each destination; see pages 8-9 for bus stations.

Buses from Hania

1 Hania—Rethimnon; daily; journey 1h (continues to Iraklion; see Timetable 2 below)

Departures from Hania: 05.30, 06.45, 07.30, 08.00 (express), 08.30, 09.00, 09.30, 10.00, 10.30, 11.00, 11.30, 12.00 (express), 12.30, 13.00, 13.30, 14.00, 14.30, 15.00, 15.30, 16.00, 16.30, 17.00, 17.30, 18.30, 19.45
Departures from Rethimnon: 07.00, 07.30 (express), 08.15, 09.15, 10.00, 10.45, 11.15, 11.45, 12.15, 13.00, 13.30, 14.00, 14.30, 15.00 (express), 15.30, 16.15, 17.00, 17.30, 18.00, 19.00, 19.30, 20.00, 20.30, 21.00

2 Hania—Iraklion (via Rethimnon); daily; journey 3h

Departures from Hania: as Timetable 1 above
Departures from Iraklion: 05.30, 06.30, 07.30, 08.15, 09.00, 09.30, 10.00 (express), 10.30, 11.15, 11.45, 12.15, 12.30 (express), 12.45, 13.15, 13.45, 14.30, 15.15, 15.45, 16.15, 16.30 (express), 16.45, 17.15, 17.45, 18.15, 18.45, 19.30

3 Hania—Omalos; daily; journey 1h20min

Departures from Hania: 06.15, 08.30, 16.30
Departures from Omalos: 07.30, 10.00, 18.00

4 Hania—Hora Sfakion; daily; journey 1h45min

Departures from Hania: 08.30, 11.00, 14.00
Departures from Hora Sfakion: 07.00, 11.00, 16.30, 18.30

5 Hania—Paleohora; daily; journey 2h

Departures from Hania: 09.00, 10.30, 12.00, 14.30, 17.00
Departures from Paleohora: 07.00, 12.00, 13.30, 15.30, 17.00

6 Hania—Sougia; daily; journey 1h30min

Departures from Hania: 09.00, 13.30
Departures from Sougia: 07.00, 14.30, 17.00

7 Hania—Kolimbari; daily; journey 50min (continues to Kasteli; see Timetable 8 below)

Departures from Hania: 06.00, 07.15, 08.30, 10.00, 11.00, 12.00, 13.00, 14.30, 15.30, 16.30, 17.30, 18.30, 20.00
Departures from Kolimbari: see Timetable 8 below and add about 20 minutes to Kasteli departure times

8 Hania—Kasteli (via Kolimbari); daily; journey 1h20min

Departures from Hania: as Timetable 7 above
Departures from Kasteli: 06.00, 07.00, 07.30, 08.00, 08.30, 09.30, 10.30, 11.30, 12.30, 14.00, 15.30, 16.15, 17.30, 19.00

9 Hania—Stalos—Agia Marina—Maleme—Chandris; daily

Departures from Hania: 06.00, 07.15, 08.00, 08.30, 09.00, 09.30, 10.00, 10.30, 11.00, 11.30, 12.00, 12.30, 13.00, 13.30, 14.30, 15.30, 16.00, 16.30, 17.00, 17.30, 18.00, 18.30, 19.00, 19.30, 20.00, 20.30, 21.30

Departures from Chandris: 08.30, 09.00, 09.15, 09.30, 10.00,
10.15, 10.30, 11.00, 11.15, 11.30, 12.00, 12.15, 16.30, 17.00,
17.30, 18.00, 18.15, 18.30, 19.00, 19.30, 19.45, 20.30, 22.30

10 Hania—Agia Galini (via Rethimnon); daily; journey 3h
Departures from Hania: 05.30, 07.30, 09.00, 10.30, 11.30,
15.30
Departures from Agia Galini: 06.45, 08.45, 10.30, 11.45, 14.45,
16.30, 19.30

11 Hania—Plakias (via Rethimnon); daily; journey 1h45min
Departures from Hania: 06.45, 07.30, 10.00, 12.30, 15.30
Departures from Plakias: 07.00, 09.30, 11.00, 12.45, 15.00,
19.15

Buses from Rethimnon

12 Rethimnon—Hania; daily; journey 1h
Departures from Rethimnon: See Timetable 1 above
Departures from Hania: See Timetable 1 above

13 Rethimnon—Iraklion; daily; journey 1h30min
Departures from Rethimnon: 06.45, 07.30 (express), 08.15,
09.00, 09.45, 10.00 (express), 10.15, 10.45, 11.45, 12.15, 12.45,
13.15, 13.45, 14.00 (express), 14.15, 14.45, 15.15, 15.45, 16.45,
17.15, 17.45, 18.15, 18.45, 19.45, 21.00
Departures from Iraklion: See Timetable 2 above

14 Rethimnon—Agia Galini; daily; journey 1h30min
Departures from Rethimnon: 06.30, 09.00, 10.30, 12.00, 14.00,
17.00
Departures from Agia Galini: As Timetable 10 above

15 Rethimnon—Plakias; daily; journey 40min
Departures from Rethimnon: 08.15, 09.30, 11.30, 13.45, 17.00
Departures from Plakias: as Timetable 11 above

**16 Rethimnon—Hora Sfakion; daily; journey 1h30min
(via Plakias)**
Departures from Rethimnon: 08.15
Departures from Hora Sfakion: 16.30

17 Rethimnon—Omalos; daily; journey 2h30min
Departures from Rethimnon: 07.00, 08.15
Departures from Omalos: via Hania; see Timetable 3 above

Buses from Kasteli (See also Timetable 8 above)

18 Kasteli—Hania—Omalos; daily; journey 3h
Departures from Kasteli: 05.00
Departures from Omalos: via Hania; see Timetable 3 above

19 Kasteli—Hania—Hora Sfakion; daily; journey 3h45min
Departures from Kasteli: via Hania; see Timetables 8 and 4 above
Departures from Hora Sfakion: 16.30

Buses from Hora Sfakion (See Timetables 4, 16, 19 above)

20 Hora Sfakion to Agia Galini; daily; journey 3h
Departures from Hora Sfakion: 16.30
Departures from Agia Galini: 08.30

Buses from Agia Galini See Timetables 10, 14, 20

Index

Geographical names comprise the only entries in this Index. For other entries, see Contents, page 3. A page number in italic type indicates a map reference; a page number in bold type indicates a photograph or sketch. Both of these may be in addition to a text reference on the same page.

Agiá (Eye-ee-**ah**) **19**, 48, *49*

Agía Fotiní (Eye-**ee**-ah Fott-een-**nee**) 36, 37

Agía Galíni (Eye-**ee**-ah Gal-**lee**-nee) **32**, 34, 35, 120
  Bus timetables 132

Agía Iríni (Eye-**ee**-ah Ee-**ree**-nee) 23, *70*, 74, 75

Agía Marína (Eye-**ee**-ah Mar-**ee**-nah) 15, 46, 47, *49*
  Bus timetables 131

Agía Rouméli (Eye-**ee**-ah Roo-**mell**-ee) 109, *111*, 112, *116*

Agía Sophiá (Eye-**ee**-ah Sof-**yah**) (Cave church near Topolia) 18, **89**, 94

Agía Triáda (Eye-**ee**-ah Tree-**ah**-dah)
  Minoan Palace near Festós 35
  Monastery on the Akrotiri Peninsula 26

Agíos Geórgios (Eye-**ee**-os Ye-**or**-yioss) (church, Anidri) 21

Agios Ioánnis (Eye-**ee**-oss Ee-o-**an**nis) 35, 37

Agios Ioánnis Gionis (chapel on the Rodopou Peninsula 79, 80, **81**, *82*

Agíos Nektários (Eye-**ee**-os Nek-**ta**-rioss) 31, 120, *121*, 124

Akrotíri (Peninsula) (Ak-roh-**tirry**) **24**, 25, 78, *82*

Alíkampos (Al-**lee**-kam-boss) 30, 33, *64*, 67

Amári (Valley) (Ah-**mar**-ee) 12, 35-7, *72*, 129

Amigdáli 64, *65*

Anídri (An-**nee**-dree) 21, *96*, 99

Apóstoli 35, 36

Aptéra (Ap-**teh**-rah) (Site) 27, 28, 30, 34

Argirimoúri 62, *65*, 66

Arméni (Ar-**menny**) 32, 34

Asféndos (As-fen-doss) *121*, 123

Askýfou (Ass-**kee**-foo) 29, 30, 120, *121*, **122-3**

Astrátigos (As-**trat**-ee-goss) **12**, *83*, 84

Chrisoskalítisas (Moní) 15, 18

Chromonastíri (Kro-mo-nas-**tirry**) *70*, 74, 76, 77

Drakónas (Dra-**ko**-nass) 28, 52, *53*

Elafonísi Islands (Ella-fon-**ee**-see) 15

Elos (**Ell**-oss) 18

Epanohóri 22, 23

Epískopi 29, 33

Falasárna (Fah-la-**sar**-nah) 16, 17

Festós (Site) (**Fay**-stoss) 34, 35

Fourfourás (For-for-**rass**) 35, 37, *127*,130

Frangokástello (Site) (Frango-**kass**-tello) 29, 31

Georgioúpoli (Yeor-**yoo**-pollee) 11, **27**, 33, 34, 62, **63**, 64, *65*, 66, 67, 68

Gerakári 35

Gíngilos (Mountain) (**Gin**-gee-loss) 100, **101**, 102,**103**, *104*, 110, *111*

Goniá (Moní) (Gon-**yah**) 15, *83*, 84, 86

Gouvernéto (Moní) (Goo-ver-**net**-toh) 12, **24**, 25, 26, 78, *82*

Gramvoúsa (Peninsula) (Gram-**voo**-sah) 16, 21, **28-9**

Haniá (Han-**ya**) **18**, 22, 25, 41, 44
  Bus timetables 131, 132
  Town plan *8*

Hóra Sfakíon (**Ho**-rah Sfak-**ee**-on) 31, 34, 109, 112, 115, *117*,118, **119**, *120*, 124
  Bus timetables 131, 132

Ida (Mountain — and range of mountains; also called Psiloritis) (**Eye**-da) 34, *127*

Imbros (**Eem**-bross) 30, 118, *121*
  Gorge 12, 30, **118**, *121*

Iráklion
  Bus timetables 131, 132

Kallérgi (Refuge in the White Mountains) (Kal-**lair**-gee) 41, **103**, *104*, 105, 106, 108

Kaloudianá 15, 16, 18

Kámbi (**Kam**-bee) 11, 28, 54, 57, *58*, 59, 60, 61

Kándanos (**Kan**-dah-noss) 19, 21

Kapadianá (Ka-pa-dee-anah) *70*, 74, 75, 76, 77

Karés (Kar-**ress**) 30, 120, *121*

Kastéli (Kass-**telly**) 12, 15, 16, 41, 44, 87, 90, 93,
  Bus timetables 131, 132

Katholikoú (Monastery, ruined) (Katholl-ee-**koo**) 26, 78, *82*

Káto Stalós (**Katto** Stal-**loss**) 15, 46, 48, *49*

Katohóri (Katto-**hor**-ee) 11, 28, 54, **55**, **56**, *58*

Katsamatádos (Katsa-mah-**tah**-doss) 12, 18, *89*, 90, **91**, 93

Kédros (Mountain) (**Keh**-dross) 35, 37, 127-8

Kolimbári (Kol-lim-**bah**-ree) 15, 79, *83*, 84, 86
Bus timetables 131
Komitádes (Kom-mee-**tah**-dess) 31, 118,
119, *121*
Korakía (Trig point on Ida Range)
(Kor-ra-**shaar**) *127*, 128, 130
Kotsifás (Gorge) (Kot-see-**fass**) 31, *124*, 125,
126
Kounoupidianá 25, 26
Kournás (Kor-**nass**) 33, *65*
Lake 11, 33, *65*, 67, 68
Kourtaliótis (Gorge) 12, 32

Láki (**Lah**-kee) 22, 24, **50**, *52*
Levká Ori (White Mountains) (Lev-**kah** O**ree**)
27, 30, 41, 54, **56**, 67, 103, 106,
109,**122-3**
Likotinará (Lik-oh-teen-ah**rah**) 63, *65*
Linoséli (col below Gíngilos) (Lee-noh-**say**-
lee) 100, 102, *104*
Lisós (Site) (Lee-**soss**) 95, 96, *97*
Loutró (Loo-**tro**) 112, **113**, 114, 115, *116*

Máleme (**Ma**-leh-meh) 15
Bus timetables 131
Marioú (Mar-ee-**oo**) 32, *124*
Mávri (Mountain) (**Mah**-vree) *105*, 106, **107**,
108
Melindaoú (Mountain) (Mel-in-dow-**oo**) *105*,
106, **107**, 108
Mesklá (Mess-**klah**) 24, 50, 51, *52*
Mírthios (**Meer**-tee-oss) 31, *124*,
125, 1266
Moni (Monastery or chapel) *see under*
Chrisoskalítisas, Goniá, Gouvernéto,
Katholikoú, Préveli
Mourí (Moo-**ree**) *89*, 92
Mourniés 27, 28
Myli (**Mee**-lee) **20**, *70*, 74, 76, 77

Néa Roúmata 22, 23
Nío Horió (**Nee**-oh Hor-**yo**) 54, 56, *59*

Omalós (Plain) (Om-ah-**loss**) 22,
24, 100, 103, *104*,109
Bus timetables 131, 132

Paleohóra (Pah-lee-oh-**horah**) 21, 23, 95,
98,99
Bus timetables 131
Plakiás (Plak-**yass**) 12, **31**, *124*, 125, 126
Bus timetables 132
Plataniás (Platan-**yas**) 15, 46, 47,
49
Polirinía (Polly-reen-**yah**) 12, 15, 16, 87, *88*,
89
Prásies 36, **69**, *71*
Prassanos (Gorge) 36, **69**, *71*, 72-3

Préveli (Monastery) (**Pre**-velly) 29, 32
Profítis Ilías (Chapel above Rethimnon) (Pro-
fee-tiss Ill-**ee**-ass) 11, *70*, 74
Psilorítis (Psill-or-**ee**-tiss) *see under* Ida

Réthimnon (**Reth**-eem-non) 11, 32, 33, 34,
35, 36, 37, 41, 44, *70*, 74, 125, 127
Bus timetables 131, 132
Town plan *9*
Rodopós (Ro-tho-**poss**) 16, 79, *82*, 83, 84
Rodopoú (Peninsula) (Rotho-**poo**) 16, 79, **81**,
82-3, 84, **85**, 86
Roussospíti (Roos-os-**spee**-tee) 11, *70*, 75

Samariá (Sah-mah-ree-**ah**) *105*, 110, *111*
Gorge **17**, 24, 100, 101, 103, *105*, **108**,
109, 110, *111*, 112, 115, *116*,
Sásalos (**Sass**-aloss) *89*, 91, **93**
Séli (**Sel**-lee) *121*,122
Sélia (near Plakiás) (**Sel**-yah) 29, 31, *124*,
125
Selía (near Georgioupoli) (Sel-**yah**) 31, 33,
64, *65*
Sirikári (Sirry-**kah**-ree) 86, 87, *88*
Soúda (Soo-dah) 26
Soúgia (**Soo**-yah) 12, 19, 21, 22, 23, 95, 96,
97, **99**
Bus timetables 131
Spíli 34
Stalós (Stah-**loss**) **26**, 46, 47, 48, *49*
Bus timetables 131
Stavrós (Stav-**ross**) **25**, 26
Stílos (**Stee**-loss) 54, 56, *59*

Thériso (**Theh**-rissoh) 11, 50, *52*, 53
Thrónos 35, 36
Topólia (Toh-**poll**-yah) 12, 15, 18, *89*, 92,
93, 94
Gorge 18, *89*, 90, 94

Váthi 15, 18
Vólika (Refuge near Kámbi in the
White Mountains) (**Voll**-ee-kah) 57, *58*,
60, **61**
Voukoliés 19, 20
Voulgáro (Vool-**gah**-roh) *89*, 92, 94
Vraskás (Vrass-**kass**) 31
Vríses (**Vree**-ses) 29, 30, 34, 37
Vríssinas (Mountain near Rethimnon) **30**, *70*,
75, 77

White Mountains *see* Levka Ori

Xilóskala (Wooden staircase leading to
Samaria Gorge) (Ksee-**loh**-ska-lah) 24,
100,102, 103, *104*, 106, 109, *111*, 115,
cover

Zoúrva (**Zoor**-vah) 51, *52*

STOP PRESS

TOWN PLANS
Hania: The road running southwest past the public gardens and zoo is renamed DIMOKRATIAS (not Konstantinou).
Rethimnon: The museum has been moved to a renovated building just outside the entrance to the fort (10 on the plan).

CAR TOURS
Petrol stations: Note that *not all petrol stations have unleaded petrol,* so if your hired car takes unleaded, fill up when you can. There is a *new petrol station in Hora Sfakion; it does* have unleaded petrol.

Tour 1: The new national road will eventually link Iraklion and Kasteli, bypassing Rethimnon, Hania, and many of the villages along the coast. At the moment there is a gap between Hania and Kolimbari. If you are heading for Stalos (Walks 1, 2), take the existing coast road. To get to the Rodopou Peninsula (Walks 13, 14), take the road signposed to Kasteli out of Kolimbari; this becomes the new national road very shortly, and you turn off right to Rodopou.

WALKS
A waymarked walk through the Agia Irini gorge (Car tour 3, at 38.5km) to Sougia was officially opened in spring 1993. At present there is no public transport, but a few companies are running coach trips. Enquire locally.

Walk 2: A blue city bus also calls at Agia. 'After you turn left in front of the large old house in Kirtomados, it's under a minute to the road, not 5 minutes... Wonderful bird-watching at the lake!... The bus stop (unmarked) on the main road is now opposite the point where the Kirtomados road joins the main road; if you are in the wrong place, the driver won't stop!' (User, 1993)

Walk 9: Users reported that in April 1993 the water in the narrowest part of the gorge was far too deep for wading, and they were forced to retrace their steps. *It is therefore recommended that this walk is only attempted in summer months.* If you wish to walk the gorge in spring, take local advice and start out very early in the morning, allowing plenty of time: you may have to retrace your steps all the way back up the gorge — a total walk of 7-8 hours.

Walk 10: On the climb to the church of Profitis Ilias, you now have to cross the main coastal road which bypasses Rethimnon (half of the hill on which the church stands has been cut away to accommodate the road). Roadworks are in progress around here, but your goal is easily seen... A concrete bridge is under construction where the path crosses the watercourse (1h from the main road in Rethimnon). (User, 1992)

Walk 11: A user reported (1992) that a new track interrupted the start of this walk, and that *the waymarking should not be followed.* Instead, follow the track to its end, where there is a concrete building. The path you want is just to the left of the building. The authors have not had an opportunity to check this.

He also pointed out that at the 40-min point, where you go left, your path traverses the north flank of Vrissinas, climbing very gently, and then zig-zags up a shallow gulley, passing the summit on the right, before heading southeast. You have to divert from the path to scramble to the summit. To leave the summit, head almost due east towards a building with water troughs; you'll easily see from there the path you climbed to reach the summit.

Walk 13: There is now a new road down to Agios Ioannis Gionis. It is north of the track shown on the map. Since the road signs direct you to Agios Ioannis Gionis along the road, it is not so easy to find the old track... 'A lovely walk, but *you must allow extra time (up to an hour!) for finding the waymarking;* if you don't find the waymarking, you are in great difficulty. The waymarking is good, but not always obvious. If you don't find it at once, you must go back to the last dot and start looking again. The arrow at a fork in the path (sometime between the 3h45min- and 5h-points) is no longer there. It's easy to lose the waymarking as you cross the first grazing area. Allow extra time here. As a guide, if you imagine that you are entering the grazing area at 6 o'clock, the way ahead is roughly at 11 o'clock... We would grade this walk as "strenuous" because of the lack of shade and the very rough going underfoot past Agios Ioannis... There are also some minor differences in the route: at the 1h15min-point there is now a large sign *on your right,* rather than in the fork, but your way is clear. Five minutes later there is now a crossroads, where we *think* you should go straight ahead. We went right, which was wrong, but we quickly picked up the route again, at the point where "the track forks a minute further on; keep up and left"... The ramshackle animal stockade is now *after* the two trees, and not before them.' (User, 1994)

Walk 14: A user reports (1993) that Moni Gonia is now *open* from 12.30 to 15.30 (just when the boc says it is closed!); we would be grateful for clarification/verification of this.

Walk 16: The bus to Kasteli (top of page 90) departs Hania at 06.00, not 06.30. To return from thi walk, take a bus coming up from Kasteli (Timetable 8 — not Timetable 1).

Walk 22: There is now a *charge to enter the gorge.*

Walk 24: There are some building works at Loutro, near the start of the ongoing path to Hor Sfakion. But you can see the path from the village. It leads off from a shrine which is visible on th hillside. To get to it, head up from the harbour, to the left of the Taverna Kri-Kri… The coastal pat (1h20min) has been widened to 1m/3ft, and is less vertiginous than previously. The authors st stress that vertigo is a possibility, with drops to the sea of 200+ feet.

Walk 25: The waymark at 2h30min is now easily seen… 'Glorious … wish it were longer! The wai out of the gorge is now easily found, as the taverna-owner has put his blue sign in front of the re waymarking arrow. There are now two tavernas as you join the road in Komitades, and you coul phone for a taxi here, rather than walk to Hora Sfakion. In winter the only bus back to Hania is a 18.00.' (User, 1994)

Walk 26: A user comments (1993) that he met a new gravel road at the 2h20min point. Has thi affected the walking route? He doesn't say.

Walk 27: In summer 1993 parts of this walk (near Mirthios) were difficult to follow, due to track an building construction.
     A user sent in this suggestion for an alternative route between Selia and Mirthios; it avoids th road section in the Kotsifas Gorge and visits an interesting watermill. We think it is preferable to th route described in the book. Leave Selia on the asphalt road leading to Mirthios. Immediatel opposite the last house in the village turn right onto the unsurfaced track you climbed from Plakia. (You will now retrace your route for some 25 minutes.) After about 15min of descent turn sharp le at a crossroads. In 5min take a right-hand fork and, in a further 5min a left-hand fork (1h15min). Thi track rounds the hillside and after a few minutes begins to enter the Kotsifas Gorge. On lookin downhill to the right, an obvious stone structure, the watermill, is easily identifiable. Shortly beyon this point, at a slight dip in the track (and just before a severely-pruned olive tree), a footpath lead off right downhill to the mill. Although slightly overgrown in places, the path is well defined. Th valley bottom is reached in about 15min. (The path heading to the right, just before the bridge, soc becomes a track and is an alternative direct route to Plakias, about 20min away.) Cross the single arch stone bridge and climb through the substantial remains of the watermill. Continue past the m on the footpath. On ascending from the mill the footpath comes onto a new track. Turn right an after about 120m/yds (some 15m/yds below a crest in the track), find your onward footpath i Mirthios climbing steeply on the left. Carry on uphill until the asphalt road is reached. You come in Mirthios at 2h05min. From here follow the notes in the book to leave Mirthios, but note that the pa beyond the parking area may be interrupted by roadworks.
     Note also: If you do not wish to visit Selia, bear right at the 28min-point in the book. Then us the notes on this Update, from the 1h15min-point, to go straight to the watermill and on Mirthios.

Walk 28: The following was received from users (1992):
     'May we make a few suggestions to clarify the route:
     (1) Advise walkers to look up at the mountain, find the deep ravine, and identify the rock spir to the left of the ravine. The path closely follows that spine, crossing it at the very beginning of th climb and then dropping down below it. The last stages, to the saddle, are in a off-shoot of th ravine. (The path can be seen very clearly from Hordaki, on Car tour 8.)
     (2) There is no view of the Amari Valley after the path drops below the spine, until the saddle i reached.
     (3) The outcrop of rock seen at 1h10min has what appears to be one holly oak with three trun. on it — the three trees are so close together. Below them is a small saddle, above the off-shoot the ravine; this is where the path forks.
     (4) There is no dab of red paint on a pine tree — all the trees are covered with a chestnut coloured lichen. However, we have placed many cairns along the route to help other walkers.'